Hetty

I hope that my book will help other children to understand the way children were treated by the Nazis, and learn about the consequences of prejudice and hatred. Hatred is a bad thing. It's a poison that eats into you. There is hatred and there is love. I like to be on the side of love.

Hetty Verolme

Hetty Verolme's stunning memoir is such an outstanding book that the judges had no hesitation in awarding it first prize. This is an important, moving and beautifully written book and deserves to become a classic — in terms of its importance as testimony and the quality of its prose, it bears comparison with *The Diary of Anne Frank.*

Judges' report, Fellowship of Australian Writers
Christina Stead Award, 2000

'a powerful and chilling account … candid and vivid.' —*The Australian*

'profoundly moving … this is an arresting book … an uplifting story.' — *Australian Book Review*

Hetty

A TRUE STORY BY
HETTY VEROLME

FREMANTLE PRESS

First published 2009 by
FREMANTLE PRESS

Original unabridged edition, *The Children's House of Belsen*, first published 2000.
This edition first published 2025.

Fremantle Press Inc. trading as Fremantle Press
PO Box 158, North Fremantle, Western Australia, 6159
fremantlepress.com.au

Cover illustration by Kadri Kuusler, kadrikuusler.com
Designed by Rebecca Mills, rebeccamills.com.au
Printed and bound in Australia by Griffin Press.

NATIONAL LIBRARY OF AUSTRALIA

A catalogue record for this book is available from the National Library of Australia

ISBN 9781760996123 (paperback)
ISBN 9781760996130 (ebook)

GOVERNMENT OF WESTERN AUSTRALIA
Department of Local Government, Sport and Cultural Industries

lotterywest

Fremantle Press is supported by the State Government through the Department of Local Government, Sport and Cultural Industries.

Fremantle Press respectfully acknowledges the Whadjuk people of the Noongar nation as the Traditional Owners and Custodians of the land where we work in Walyalup.

FSC www.fsc.org
MIX
Paper | Supporting responsible forestry
FSC® C018684

I dedicate this book
to my grandchildren
Jacleen Sarah Ray
and Adam Maurice Passman
with love from their Oma

Foreword

In 2024, we lost Hetty, whose absence leaves an enormous void in our lives. Soon, we will have lost all direct witnesses to the Holocaust's atrocities and without dedicated effort, their memories risk fading. Among so many achievements, Hetty worked tirelessly to ensure that we 'Never Forget' the Holocaust. More than that, she hoped her story would promote and inspire strength and resilience in the next generation. Hetty wanted us all to know that even in our darkest times, 'tomorrow will be a better day'. Though she is no longer with us, her message must endure. We, her family, have pledged to carry forward this important work. By reading this book, you help to continue her legacy. From the bottom of our hearts, we thank you for joining us in this effort and contributing to a brighter future.

With love,
Julia, Jackie and Adam

Hetty with her brothers, Max and Jack, 1941.

Prologue

I did not have a carefree childhood. I spent years of my childhood in Belsen concentration camp in Germany, deported there by the Germans during World War II with my father and mother, and my two brothers.

If I were to tell you of the experiences of all our family this book would never come to an end, so I will confine myself to telling you the true story of my experiences in the Children's House of Belsen.

Chapter 1

My family lived in Amsterdam, in the Jewish quarter. It never used to be a Jewish quarter. The Dutch people did not know the word 'segregation', and everybody could live wherever they wanted. Religion and belief were not considered an issue. Then, in 1941, during the German occupation of Holland, the Germans decided to concentrate the Jewish population in Amsterdam East.

In February 1941 the Germans raided the city market of Amsterdam in retaliation for the killing of a Dutch Nazi officer in a fight the previous day. Four hundred men were picked up and herded into trucks. Unfortunately, my father's favourite cousin, Simon, was one of the men. Although we heard rumours, we had no idea where the men were taken. In May 1941 my father received a postcard marked Mauthausen. Simon wrote:

Dear Maurice and family
I am in Mauthausen and the work is not bad. I hope

Hetty's shadow falls over children from her street as she photographs them. All of the children were sent to Auschwitz where they died in the gas chamber, 1942.

From left, back row: Iesy Gerritse, unknown.
Front row: Siena Soep, Nathan Smeer, Betty Smeer.

that everything is good with all of you. Please give my regards to Dozeman, and is Spitty still alive?
Simon

As we knew the card had to pass through the German censor, there must be a hidden message. For two days my father walked through the house in his pyjamas with the card in his hand trying to decode the message. On the second day he came to me in the kitchen and said, 'I know what Simon wants to tell us. Dozeman is the name of the baker around the corner; Spitty is the name of our dog. So, what he is really trying to say is that he is very hungry and that it is a dog's life in Mauthausen.'

We realised then that the Germans would be without mercy in their plans to eradicate the Jewish population in Holland. My father looked at me with worried eyes and said, 'I must do everything in my power to prevent us being sent to Germany.'

There were many raids in the Jewish quarter during the summer of 1942. We saw families dragged from their homes, never to be heard of again. Some of these people were crying when they were taken away; others were relieved that the waiting was over. We watched through the curtains as the Germans marched long columns of people down the street to the station, where the trains would take them far away from the things they loved and lived for. My family felt very sad after each raid. No one knew what was happening to our friends and relatives.

We had been very lucky. My father was a well-to-do textile merchant. When the raids started, someone told him that we could buy our freedom from the German SS Commander Aus der Funten in the form of a work deportation exemption. We could then be exchanged for German prisoners of war via Portugal.

My father did not hesitate. He sold most of our valuables and managed to get about five hundred thousand guilders together. The question was, who was going to approach Commander Aus der Funten at SS headquarters? This was dangerous — many people had gone there and not returned. After a long discussion, Mum persuaded Dad to let her go. She reasoned that a woman might have a better chance of being admitted.

On the sunny morning of 22 September 1942, my mother set out to walk the eight miles to try to save her family. Jews were not permitted to travel on buses or trams. All day we lived a nightmare, trying not to think of all the things that might happen to our mother. The day dragged on, until at five o'clock the telephone rang. After some hesitation my father picked up the receiver, afraid of what he might hear, but his face transformed into a smile. Mum was all right and on her way home. She had spoken to Commander Aus der Funten, and was told to come back with the money and our passports the next week. Our spirits lifted. Soon we might live in freedom again, without being shunned or hunted down.

The week passed and Mum set out once more for SS headquarters, but this time she came home earlier, with photocopies of our precious passports, stamped by order of Commander Aus der Funten: *The holder of this passport is exempt from work deportation.* The work deportation exemption protected us from being taken away during the raids which went on night after night. And we desperately wanted to believe the verbal promise that we would be exchanged for prisoners of war.

My mother's mother lived just down the street from us. She was the most wonderful person, loved by the entire neighbourhood. Everyone called her Oma (Grandma) Judy. My wonderful grandmother; she looked after us like no one else.

On Friday, 2 October 1942, Oma cooked a sweet pear cake. 'Eat well, my children, and may God bless you all. I am sure it is the last time I will cook for you,' Oma said. 'I can feel it. Tonight they will come to get me.'

'Please Oma, don't talk like that.' I was in tears. 'If you do feel like this, stay with us tonight. Don't go home — if you do go, I'm coming with you.'

'No.' Oma was firm. 'Tonight you sleep at home.'

Sometimes I slept at Oma's place so she would not be so lonely at night, even though it was forbidden by the Germans to stay the night in someone else's home. (The

Germans had declared a curfew from eight o'clock at night until six in the morning for the entire Dutch population.)

Before eight o'clock, Oma kissed us all with tears in her eyes and said, 'Be good, my children. I love you all very much.' With those words she left.

From that moment Mum stationed herself in front of the bedroom window where she could see Oma's street. The Germans started to arrive at about quarter past eight. The raid was on. Through the curtains we could see them going from door to door to bring people out of their homes. I was in the living room when my father called out, 'Run to the bedroom, they've got Oma! Be quick and you can say goodbye.'

From the bedroom window we could see Oma with her bags, waving and calling to us.

'Mother, Mother!' Mum screamed. She opened the window, although that was strictly forbidden, and leant out, waving frantically. 'God, don't let them take my mother.'

My father grabbed her and pulled her back inside. The Germans motioned Oma to move on.

'Goodbye my children,' Oma called while she walked. 'Goodbye, goodbye.'

They were the last words we heard from Oma. My lovely sweet grandmother. We had heard people calling goodbye many times before, but this time the Germans had hit our family. That terrible Friday night I will never forget as long as I live.

Months passed but the Germans did not let up on the raids. Our neighbourhood became very quiet. The houses were empty because when the Germans picked up people, a few days later Puls, a carrier company contracted by the Germans, would come and take their furniture and belongings. All the goods from Jewish homes were sent to Germany.

Our school in the President Brandt Straat also emptied. Most of the students had been deported to Germany and Jewish teachers replaced all the gentile teachers.

On Sunday, 20 June 1943, I was awake early. Suddenly I heard announcements from cars with loudspeakers, ordering Jews to get ready for immediate transportation. The whole neighbourhood was sealed off by the SS so no one could escape. The rest of the residents were told to stay indoors. Heavily armed police went from door to door checking passports and other documents. They drove the people out of their homes to an area right across from our home. The people were forced into an enormous queue and guarded by German soldiers with drawn bayonets. For five hours the people, young and old, stood huddled together without food or water, until they were ordered to start walking to Amstel Station, where they would board a train for Westerbork. The whole city of Amsterdam was raided that day and only a few families were allowed to stay. Our family was one of them.

During 1943 my father's parents went into hiding, and a man from the Dutch Resistance came occasionally to tell us how they were. He would bring us letters and news about the War.

As a textile merchant, my father was still allowed to trade during all this upheaval. Shortly after the German occupation, every Jew who was in business was ordered to register the business and apply for a licence to operate. My father was well-established — his large stalls with magnificent fabrics were well known in the markets of Amsterdam. He held two different licences, one for the markets and the other for wholesale business. For a while everything seemed all right; it was business as usual. Then came the order that everyone with two licences had to surrender one. Mum and Dad debated for days and finally decided to send the market licence for renewal and surrender the wholesale licence.

It was a lucky choice. The people who had kept their wholesale licences were not so lucky. Their businesses were confiscated by the Germans, and they were left with nothing. Once-wealthy people had no money to buy food for their families. They came to visit our home in the afternoons and soon devised a plan: my father would buy more goods than he needed for his own business and allow them to sell the surplus so they could make some money in order to eat. Of course, we had to do this very carefully in case traitors reported us to the SS.

Our attic soon became a warehouse where rolls of fabric were neatly stacked on shelves. It was there that I escaped early in the mornings to do my homework. One morning at about five o'clock, as I was climbing the stairs to the attic, I met a man carrying down rolls of material. I didn't like something in his manner and asked him his name. 'Jan,' he told me as he raced down the stairs. Suspicious, I ran up to the attic. The locks on the door were broken and only a few rolls of material were left lying on the floor. The room that had been chock-a-block full was empty. I ran into my parents' bedroom and blurted out that we had been robbed.

My father rushed into the street in his pyjamas in an effort to catch the thief, to no avail. Dad was furious and went to ring the police.

My mother became very worried and said, 'Don't do this, Maurice. It can be very dangerous to bring attention to us as Jews. Better forget about it.'

But my father was so mad he did not want to think about the consequences. Two Dutch policemen arrived about half an hour later. Dirk was elderly, but Henny was a very tall young man with blond hair and sparkling blue eyes. Henny asked me questions about what the man looked like, what he had said to me, and other details about what had happened. He was such a nice policeman that by the time he had finished questioning me, I adored him as only a young girl can.

When I returned home from school that afternoon, my father told me that they had caught the thief. Most of the goods had been recovered and returned.

Henny became a good friend of our family's and he would often drop in after his afternoon shifts. If I happened to be home, he would give me one of his beautiful smiles and say, 'How is little Hetty today? Did you do your best at school?'

He was such a wonderful person — his smile, the open look of his eyes. Everybody loved him. One day I came home from school and found my father and Henny in serious conversation.

I heard Henny say, 'No, Maurice, not this time. First we'll see if they arrive safely. I tell you what we'll do. Tear a hundred guilder banknote in two and I'll give one half to the doctor who is going with his family and ask him to post it back to Amsterdam when they arrive in Switzerland. When the half of the banknote arrives, we'll know they've arrived safely and you and your family can go on the next trip.'

Reluctantly my father agreed. He took out his wallet, pulled out a one-hundred guilder note and tore it in two.

He handed one half to Henny and carefully put the remaining half back in his wallet.

Henny got up to leave, then noticed me for the first time. He didn't smile. He looked strained and tense. I remained silent.

'Good luck, Henny. Be careful,' my father said, and extended his hand.

When Henny had gone, my father confided in me what it was all about. The Dutch Resistance, of which Henny was a member, believed they had found an escape route. A barge would take thirty people up the river Rhine through Germany to Switzerland. The people would be hidden below the deck.

'I wanted us to be on the barge,' Dad said, 'but Henny wants us to wait for the next trip.'

I was glad Henny didn't want us to go, and I told my father so. 'It's much too dangerous. The idea of going through Germany scares me.'

'Yes,' Dad said. 'I understand that.' He let out a deep sigh. 'We must wait to see if that doctor sends the banknote from Switzerland. I do hope so, for his sake.'

'When is the boat going?' I asked.

'In two days,' Dad said.

Four days went by. We had expected Henny to come but he didn't. Dad was nervous and we were worried as well. On the fifth day, Dirk, the elderly policeman, came to see us. He told us that he had heard Henny had been arrested by the SS two days previously and taken to the SS headquarters. We were appalled; we knew about the atrocities committed there by the SS. Dirk told us that as far as he had been able to find out, thirty people had boarded the barge. They had paid large amounts of money to the crew, and the barge had left early in the night. At about midnight, the crew started to throw the families overboard. Their screams of terror were so loud that a German patrol boat came to investigate and everyone was rounded up, with disastrous results for Henny. Dirk told us that Henny was in hospital under SS guard.

'My family owes their lives to Henny. He advised me not to go on this trip but to wait,' my father said, his face ashen. 'How can I thank him enough for stopping me from doing something foolish. Oh God! Let him get better!' He banged his fist on the table. 'Please,' he repeated, 'let him get better.'

But Henny was in a very bad condition. The SS had beaten his head into a bloodied mess and whipped him until his kidneys had ruptured. Mercifully our wonderful, courageous Henny passed away the next day.

The Germans had checked our passports a few times by now, but left our house after seeing the exemption stamps on them. We had heard no more about our trip to

Portugal, but our suitcases remained packed under our beds in case the summons came. On 29 September 1943, at four o'clock in the morning, the doorbell began ringing urgently, accompanied by loud banging on the front door. The banging woke everyone in the house.

I heard my parents moving about in their bedroom, my mother saying, 'They're here, they're here.' From my bedroom I could see into the hall. I saw my mother open the door and there stood an SS officer and a German soldier with a drawn bayonet.

'Jews?' the officer asked.

My mother nodded.

'Passports,' he snapped, 'quick.'

My father had already appeared with the passports, sure that the stamp would do its magic work again. Confidently he handed over the passports to the SS officer, who examined them carefully and ordered all five of us to line up in the hall. There we stood in our pyjamas, my mother holding her pink dressing-gown tightly around herself. The SS officer told the soldier to keep watch over us while he had a look around to see if there was anyone else.

We silently prayed. In the confusion we had forgotten that my mother's cousin, Morris, and my father's niece, Sonja, were in the house. To top it off, Morris had been hiding for a year; he had arrived only the day before. He had no passport or papers. Sonja had a Jewish mother and a gentile father, and had papers to prove it. While the SS officer searched the house, we held our breath. We could hear him opening doors and banging them closed again. The soldier stayed in front of us with his drawn bayonet.

The officer returned with Sonja. He had found her in the sitting room. We were all wondering what had happened to Morris. Why hadn't the SS officer found him? We tried to talk to each other with our eyes, wanting to know the answer to this unbelievable thing, but we weren't left with much time to ponder over it.

'Your papers?' the SS officer asked Sonja.

She handed them to the officer.

'So you are half-Jew. What are you doing in this house? It is forbidden to stay overnight in someone else's quarters.' By this time, he had worked himself into a temper. 'Answer me!' he shouted.

We all froze, looking at Sonja and the officer. Sonja was very pale, but proudly held her head up high and looked the officer straight in the face. Softly she said that during the day she had paid us a visit, and by the time the curfew came around she had a migraine headache, and it had been impossible for her to get home safely.

'You're lying!' the officer screamed. 'I'll keep your passport and you will come with the rest of them to the station. There someone higher than me will deal with you.'

The officer turned to us and said, 'Jews, I'll give you one

hour to get ready.' He ordered the German soldier to watch us carefully until he returned to take us to the station.

My mother told us all to get dressed. 'We don't know where we're going, so dress warmly.' She pushed Max and Jacky in front of her towards their room.

Sonja and I said nothing. Mum came back down the hall, and in her eyes, we could see that Morris was okay. She drew us all into the main bedroom. Whispering, she told us that when the Germans banged on the door, Morris had hidden himself under the bed among the suitcases. He had a bad moment when the officer searched the room, but he didn't look under the bed.

'What's Morris going to do now?' Max asked Mum.

'I told him to stay where he is until after we're gone, and to give our neighbours any valuables that are left. It's better that they have it than Puls,' Mum said.

After I got dressed I went to find Max and Jacky, and the three of us went to my parents' room. In the hall, we had to pass the German soldier, who by that time was tired of holding his bayonet. He'd placed it against the wall and was leaning beside it.

Dad was sitting on the side of the bed. He looked very upset. 'Children, I'm very sorry this has happened,' he said. 'I've done everything I could so we didn't have to go to Germany. I gave nearly all our money to the SS to save you. I'm very, very sorry.' By now Dad was crying and we all tried to tell him it was not his fault. He hushed us and said, 'We don't know what's going to happen, but you must promise me faithfully that if you are alive when this terrible war is over, no matter where you are, you must try your utmost to come back to Amsterdam, to the Pomstra family, around the corner. They have some shares and some jewels that I gave them to keep until after the war. Even if your mother or I don't return, they've promised they will look after you. Now, children, do you all understand that?'

The three of us nodded our heads.

'Come here,' Dad said. He held us close. 'I'm sorry, I'm so sorry,' he kept repeating.

Mum put her hand on Dad's shoulder. 'Come on,' she said. 'The SS officer will be back any minute.' Reluctantly, Dad let us go, and we followed Mum into the kitchen.

It was half-past six when the SS officer returned.

My mother was the last one to leave our apartment. She locked the front door firmly. Nobody spoke as we descended the stairs to the street. When we were all down, the SS officer told us to wait in the porch. It was a beautiful morning — the sun was shining and the square was deserted — except for the trucks waiting to take us to the station.

'*Psst.*'

My mother and I heard the soft sound, and we turned to see where it was coming from. The door next to our apartment was opened a slit and our neighbour was peering through it. Mum and I moved closer to the door.

'What's going on?' the neighbour asked. 'Did the bastards come to take you away?'

Mum nodded and rummaged in her handbag. She took out the keys to our house and handed them to the neighbour.

'Here,' she said. 'After we've gone, go inside and help Morris, who is hiding upstairs. Also, take whatever you want.'

'Leave it to me,' our neighbour said. 'In the meantime, look after yourselves. Let's hope that this lousy war will soon be over. Good luck.' Silently, he closed the door.

The SS officer returned with another family.

'Start walking!' he ordered, and we all set out towards the trucks.

How strange the square looks, I thought, as we were crossing the road. This could not be the same square I had crossed a thousand times on my way to school. But then, would anything be the same again? We arrived at the parked trucks and were ordered to get in quickly. We all scrambled on board and stood up in the back with the guard. We could hear the SS officer laughing and joking in the front cabin with the driver. Yes, they could laugh!

The truck arrived at the station and we filed inside. The SS officer marched Sonja away. Although there were about a thousand people altogether, an unnatural hush lay over the hall. We made conversation only in whispers. It looked like all the remaining Jews in Amsterdam had been picked up in the raid. We soon found out that even the Jewish Council President, Abraham Asscher, and Councillor Abraham Soep and their families had been picked up. More and more people were being brought to the station. By eight o'clock the hall looked like an ant hill. People — young and old, babies and children — were all huddled together. Rumours started to circulate. Some said we were going to Portugal, others that Hitler had sent orders that all the Jews left in Amsterdam were to be killed. We didn't know what to believe. We were torn between hope and despair.

Time moved on. By nine o'clock we were still in the station hall. The only SS guards were outside the station. We could see Sonja standing with her hands behind her back and her face to the wall. We did not go near her because we were afraid that might make it worse for her, so we waved from a distance. The same thought was in everyone's mind: When would the train come?

'Hetty,' I heard a voice calling. I turned around to see my special boyfriend. I had been at school with Herman for years. He had carried my school case, and at the local gym we always teamed up together.

'Herman! Did they get you too?'

'Yes,' he said. 'We've been here since three o'clock.'

'How's your mother? Is she all right?' I asked.

'Mum's all right,' Herman said, 'but Dad's taking it pretty rough. I'll tell you something funny. There's a man down there who's telling everybody that the train isn't coming because it's got a flat tyre.'

We laughed. It was good to laugh in the midst of all this misery.

'Do you know where we're going?' I asked.

'I think we're going to Westerbork. Listen, Hetty, if you have a chance on the train, ask your mother to cut your hair short, because when we arrive in Westerbork you have to pass a health test by a German doctor. If he thinks your hair isn't clean enough, they shave it all off.'

I was heartbroken. My hair! But before I could reply a whistle started blowing, and a voice came over the address system asking for silence. The hall became very quiet. No one moved. This was the moment. You could feel the tension rising. Then the voice said: 'Jews, we want you to pick up your luggage and proceed to platform three, where the train will take you to Westerbork. Group A will come forward first. Group B will follow, and so on.'

It was chaos in the big hall. People were running everywhere to return to their groups. Mothers were looking for their children, and fathers struggled with the luggage for whole families. Already groups A and B were passing through the turnstiles, and C and D were following. We were with group W, so we were not so pressed for time.

When group S went by, Herman called out, 'Hetty, see you in Westerbork. Remember what I told you.'

Herman Soesman, Hetty's school sweetheart.
He died in Auschwitz on 22 October 1943.

Then Mum said to me. 'Hetty, you look after Jacky so that we don't lose him. We must try to keep close together.'

I took Jacky firmly by the hand.

'That's it,' Dad said, 'they've just called out our letter. Let's go, and God be with us.'

There was a tremendous crush at the turnstiles, but we managed to reach the platform together. It was the longest train I had ever seen. The locomotive was already a long way out of the station. As each carriage filled up, it moved further forward. We were lucky because it was a passenger train, not the cattle wagons used to transport most of the people.

Westerbork was what the Germans called Durchgangslager, which means repatriation camp. From there, people were sent to different camps in Germany — Sachsenhausen, Buchenwald, Ravensbrück, Dachau, Neuengamme, Mauthausen and Oranienburg. In Poland it was Auschwitz, Birkenau, Sobibor, Blechhammer, Gleiwitz and Monowitz. The Germans had told the Jewish population in Holland that we would be put to work in the camps with plenty of food and family accommodation. Now we were on our way. Slowly, the train left the Amstel Station. In our compartment there were only about thirty people. We were lucky. At least we all had a seat. Silently we watched the passing scenery, the fields, the cows, the orchards. *What now, what now?* sang the wheels of the train.

Sonia Santiel, one of Hetty's school friends, with the yellow Star of David the Jewish population in Holland were forced to wear. Sonia was among the first to be sent to Auschwitz, where she died.

Chapter 2

Our first glimpse of Westerbork was a long platform with barracks next to it. First of all we had to be registered, and we also had to declare if we had any precious jewels, gold or money with us. This was our first encounter with the rigid registration system the Germans maintained.

Hours and hours passed. One thousand six hundred people had to be checked in and we were some of the last. It was eleven o'clock at night and we were very tired. At last it was all over and we were taken to barrack seventy. Our luggage was already in the entrance hall. The left side of the barrack housed the women and children, and the right side was the men's dormitory. The beds were very close together and the bunks were three beds high. My mother and I each occupied a top bunk, Jacky had the bed under mine, and Max was with Dad on the other side of the barrack. There were no sheets on the beds, only a grey blanket and a straw mattress. Exhausted, we slept.

The next morning we were woken up at seven o'clock. Every muscle in my body was complaining, but we had to make a move as coffee and bread would be served in fifteen minutes.

After breakfast, we decided to explore Westerbork. We found a small hospital, workshops and a factory. What they produced, we didn't know.

We soon found that life in Westerbork was not too bad, but we had to do without conveniences like showers and privacy. Although the food was not very appetising, you could receive parcels from friends to supplement your rations.

Sonja, who had been released by the SS, began sending us parcels of food, so we had enough to eat. She also sent a warm coat for me and a pair of warm slacks for each of us. The days passed. I had met Herman a few days after arriving in Westerbork. He and his parents were in barrack sixty-eight. We spent as much time together as we could.

About six weeks after our arrival in Westerbork, we heard that a transport of people was going to be sent away to Germany. Early one morning a list of names was hung in the entrance hall of the barrack. Whoever had their name on the list had to be ready with their luggage by seven o'clock that night. From six o'clock, everybody would be confined to barracks.

That whole day was bedlam in the camp. Families who

were being separated were crying. A notice in the hall advised that Rabbi Blum would bless anyone if they were in need of it. Young and old were queuing up to be blessed. I went as well, and as long as I live I will never forget the kind eyes that looked into mine before I bowed my head to receive my blessing.

At seven o'clock, two guards came for the people who had to go on the train. It was a cattle train and on the roof of the cars were machine-guns to prevent anyone escaping during the journey. How can one express the misery of having to farewell those who were leaving?

At about eight o'clock a parcel arrived for me — a watch with a photograph of Herman on the dial face and a Swann fountain pen, one of his valued possessions. I cried. My heart was breaking to have us parted in such a cruel manner, and my mother closed her arms around me to soften the pain.

At midnight the train left. Herman and his parents and Rabbi Blum were on the train. I learnt much later they were taken to Auschwitz and died in the gas chamber.

A few weeks after that horrible night, a transport of about one hundred people arrived. Soon we found out that my father's parents were with them. My father obtained a pass to visit them, and there he heard a pitiful story. My grandparents had been paying the people who were hiding them, and when the money ran out, the horrible people

Hetty's cousins, Millicent and Max. Together with their parents, Phillip and Branka van Kamerik, they were on the last transport to Auschwitz in September 1944.
On arrival they were sent to the gas chambers.

delivered them straight to the Germans.

The following Sunday we were permitted to see my grandparents. My grandmother's hair had turned white and she was a ghost of her former self, she had become so thin.

'My darling,' she said, 'how much you have grown.' She held me tightly in her arms, tears streaming down her face.

'Please Oma, don't cry,' I begged.

'Here young lady, don't I get a kiss, too?' asked Opa.

Oma let me go. I ran over to Opa and embraced him. He was skinny as well, but he still had a twinkle in his eye. My grandfather was always a cheerful, happy-go-lucky person. We stayed all Sunday afternoon together. We had brought food and clothing for them because they had nothing. During the few weeks my grandparents stayed in Westerbork, we visited them as many times as we were allowed, until, on 25 January 1944, they were sent away to Auschwitz.

The fifth of December is St Nicholas' Day in Holland. This is the day that young children receive presents if they have been good all year round. Three weeks before I had put the children in the barrack to work making streamers from coloured paper and glue. We also made trains and cars out of matchboxes as presents for themselves. A spirit of goodwill pervaded the barrack. People would stop by the table where the little ones worked to give advice and help out. The pile of presents grew until every child had a gift.

The women of the barrack had put themselves to work too, and fashioned a bishop's robe and mitre. One of the fathers would act as St Nicholas. Every child went to bed early the night before St Nicholas' Day — St Nicholas did not like naughty children who went to bed late.

There was great activity on the morning of 5 December 1943. Some women were making cookies and others were making sweets. The men also got into the act, shifting bunks to make room for chairs. A special chair was decorated for St Nicholas. The colourful streamers the children had made were hung from the ceiling. Everybody was excited. By now the news had spread that barrack seventy was having a party. We had many visitors that day from the other barracks.

At six o'clock that night the children were sitting in their best clothes, waiting for St Nicholas. A loud knocking on the door heralded his arrival. 'It's St Nicholas,' everyone whispered, and the children began to sing, 'Welcome, St Nicholas.' In the doorway stood St Nicholas, and he had brought his helper Black Peter with him. He was carrying the large sack containing all the presents. Just seeing the children's faces, their eyes sparkling, was reward enough for the weeks of work.

At eight o'clock the children went to bed, but the party was not yet over. The adults gathered around the piano we had borrowed and began singing. Everyone looked happy for the first time in a long time. The barrack elder,

Walter, climbed onto a chair and asked for silence.

'Ladies and gentlemen,' he said, 'I would like to pay tribute to a young girl within our midst, who has, by her own initiative, given us much happiness today.'

He motioned me to come near him. 'Hetty, I'm proud to know you, and I'm sure that I express the wish of everyone here that you and your family may come through these trying times safe and healthy, and that you may grow up into a beautiful young lady. As a memento of this occasion, I would like you to accept this mirror in gratitude from us all, and may you see yourself grow prettier still as time goes by.'

Walter kissed me on both cheeks and gave me a hand mirror with a pink bow. Loud applause filled the room. I had never been praised in public before, and I did not know where to look or what to say.

Christmas came and went; 1944 had arrived. What would this year bring? The hope that it would end our misery was in everyone's hearts. No transport had gone during the festive season, but we knew it would not be long now.

On 10 January 1944, a transport of eight hundred people went to Bergen-Belsen. On 1 February 1944 our name was on the list. That night, with a thousand other people, we boarded the train. We left Westerbork and travelled through the night. We tried to get some sleep during the journey but it was impossible. The uncertainty of our fate kept us awake.

The train finally drew to a halt. 'Celle' was the name on

the signpost. Then I heard Dad's shocked exclamation: 'Oh, dear God, help us!' On the platform, there were about thirty SS men with bloodhounds straining on their leashes.

'Get out!' someone screamed.

Bewildered, we left the train.

'Leave your luggage except for hand luggage, and line up,' an SS officer shouted.

A long queue formed. Mothers held onto their children. Some of the men, including Dad, were told to come forward and pack the luggage onto trucks. The long columns of people started to move.

We walked and walked and walked. We had all taken some small bags with us. Those bags became as heavy as lead during the long walk. Our feet were dragging, and the speed of the columns had slowed down.

Behind us the SS were shouting, 'Hurry up, hurry up!'

Where were we going? Would we ever get there? How long would it take? At least the road was made of bitumen, which was a blessing. We did not meet a soul. There were no cars, no people, only the guards and their dogs. If the circumstances had not been so miserable, we might have enjoyed the beauty of the surrounding forest. The hours passed and we were still walking. Then at last we could see a high fence of barbed wire and a gate. On the other side was an office where SS guards were sitting. About six hundred metres further to the left, we passed through another gate: we had arrived in Bergen-Belsen concentration camp.

Chapter 3

Our first impression of Belsen was of a big, open place. About thirty barracks were neatly built in rows of three or four, with about twenty-foot wide streets in between. Everything looked neat and tidy. When we arrived, Belsen was a camp for prisoners of war, not the horror camp it later became. It was about one kilometre square, and divided into smaller camps. Our camp was the Sternlager, or 'Star Camp', because all the Jewish population in Holland were forced to wear the yellow Star of David. Surrounding the entire place was a strip of land about twenty yards wide, dotted with skull-and-crossbones warning signs. High wire fences with watchtowers marked the perimeter.

We were received by Herr Albela, our camp elder, a Greek man who had been in Belsen for about eight weeks. Herr Albela spoke to us in German, which was translated by one of our men. He told us that the gate between the men's and women's section would close at eight o'clock at night. During the day, we could be together. It was the same as in Westerbork.

Our barrack was divided into three sections: the dining room, with large tables and chairs around them; a dormitory; and a combined laundry and washhouse. The dormitory had plenty of windows for air and light. The washhouse had a cement floor with about ten washbasins, a row of laundry troughs and ten toilets. The first thing we did was to sit down and kick off our shoes. Did our feet hurt! Especially mine. Two days before we left Westerbork, I had dropped a pan of boiling water over my foot, and now it was red and swollen.

After we had rested for a while, we went to find our beds. Mum had not said a word about Dad, but I knew she was worried. We had not seen him since we arrived, and now it was about four o'clock. We were brought a large container of soup. It smelled good. The walk had made us hungry and we hadn't eaten since the day before, but after trying one spoonful I looked at Mum. I could see that she didn't like it either. It was just hot water, with a thread of sauerkraut floating in it here and there. We couldn't eat it and we were not alone. One lady decided to wash her feet with the soup, an action which was soon followed by others in our barrack.

It was about half-past four when the truck carrying our luggage arrived. The men who had been ordered to stay behind at the station had loaded the luggage of all the thousand people who had arrived at Celle that morning. Everybody hurried to what became known as the

Appelplatz, the place where rollcall was held. We were just in time to see my father enter the camp sitting on top of the luggage on the truck.

Everybody surged forward to collect their belongings. We had sheets and blankets with us, and we stuffed jumpers in a pillowslip to make do for pillows. We put our suitcase with the rest of our clothing on top of Jacky's bed near the foot end. This way we could keep an eye on it.

Earlier that day two men had entered our barrack and asked if anyone spoke German. A skinny lady of about forty came forward. She was a refugee who had been given asylum in Holland in 1937. Although we couldn't understand much of what was being said, we gathered that she had been appointed as our barrack elder. When the men left, she took control as if she had done it all her life, allocating cupboards and giving instructions.

At about seven o'clock, Max and Dad left for their barrack and did not return until the next morning.

Our barrack was the last to be occupied and although it had sixty beds, only thirty people were there. The barrack was new and the bunks only two-high. The straw mattresses were also new. There was a single row of beds along the length of the wall and windows, and double rows of beds in the middle of the dormitory.

No food was brought to us that first night, so Mum gave us some biscuits. We were so tired that by eight o'clock everybody was in bed.

At first light the next morning, we awoke and surveyed our new surroundings. Although it was winter the sun was shining, which gave the dormitory a friendly atmosphere. Mum, Jacky and I set out with towels and soap. The washhouse was empty except for one elderly lady who was standing naked at a washbasin. I had never seen a stranger naked before and it shocked me deeply. The woman took no notice of us and continued to wash herself. My God, I thought, do all women look like this when they grow old? The woman was tall and very skinny. Her skin was yellow and very dry. Her breasts, like empty paper bags, drooped right down to her waist.

My mother, seeing the astonishment in my eyes, whispered, 'Don't look. Give the woman some privacy.'

Jacky was also visibly shocked, but Mum turned him away firmly and told him to start washing himself. Jacky and I could not help ourselves. Our eyes wandered over to the woman, who, after a while, started to dry herself firmly and then, with a quick movement, threw her breast over her shoulder to dry the front part of her body. This became too much even for my mother. With our faces and hands still wet, she practically pushed us out of the washhouse. Once outside, the three of us burst into laughter and Jacky immediately dubbed the woman 'Mrs Cow'. The woman had shown no shame or embarrassment when we saw her naked, and we had to accept that our own inhibitions would no longer be considered. Although we did not realise it at the time, this encounter was the start of the degeneration of our values which we were to experience during our years in Belsen.

When we got back to the barrack we were told that coffee had arrived, but when we tasted it, it was awful. It was only brown-coloured water.

Max and Dad arrived at about nine o'clock. Their barrack was crowded and they told us that the Chief Rabbi was with them. Mum and Dad arranged with our barrack elder to receive the daily rations for Dad and Max in our barrack. This way we could remain a family unit.

For a few days, the SS left us in peace. Everybody tried to settle in and adjust to the daily routine in Belsen. After about three days, our barrack elder advised us that we all had to attend rollcall at seven o'clock sharp the next morning.

Everyone was up by six. We had a quick wash and dressed as warmly as we could, then went to the dining room where we received a beaker of the warm brown water. At half-past six, the messengers started calling, 'Everyone to rollcall.' Everyone who could walk, even children as young as three, had to go to the Appelplatz to be counted.

We stood in rows of five, and when the Scharführer came to count us, we had to stand to attention with our heads up and eyes straight ahead. No movement or sound was allowed. We weren't used to lining up like an army or being counted like criminals. We were lucky that first morning. Either the figures were correct or the SS had something better to do, but they let us get away after one-and-a-half hours. The next day we were not so lucky. That time they kept us for two hours at rollcall.

Soon we found out that if we did not come 'up to standard', the SS would let us stand at the Appelplatz for hours on end. The barrack elders desperately tried to train us to behave the way the SS wanted. The agonising hours at the Appelplatz went by very slowly, and many a prayer went up from elderly people near death on their feet and children shivering from cold and hunger, their little faces becoming more pinched as the days went by. Sometimes it was way past lunchtime before the SS let us go. Herr Albela would blow a whistle — the music of an orchestra could not have sounded sweeter — and we would run as quickly as our legs could carry us back to the barracks. Our beds had become our home, the only place we felt a little safe.

We had been in Belsen for about a week when the SS ordered all the men, some as young as fifteen, to come to rollcall at dawn to form work units. One of the toughest jobs belonged to the unit that went outside the camp into the woods to dig out the roots of tree stumps. It was hard and merciless work. My father and the Chief Rabbi were picked for this unit. They would leave the camp early and only return late in the afternoon.

Then the women were summoned to rollcall. From them, the SS selected groups to work in the kitchens to cook the food for the camp. Mum was picked to work in the peel kitchen. She had to get up at three to go to rollcall and then start work at four and work all day. I had the task of looking after my brothers — washing their clothing, making their beds and collecting our daily food rations.

After about three weeks in Belsen the burns on my foot had still not healed and the wound looked inflamed. The camp doctor advised me to rest for a week and gave me a letter so I did not have to attend rollcall. I was quite happy to stay in bed reading. Everybody else had gone to rollcall except another woman, who was sick in bed.

After about two hours, the women and children returned from rollcall, and soon after that our lunch arrived. It wasn't busy in the peel kitchen, so my mother had worked only a few hours before returning to the barrack. I decided to get up and join her for a while in the dining room. As I pulled out a chair, we heard planes approaching, and machine-guns from the watchtowers going into action. Everybody was screaming. I panicked and started to run back to my bed. Bullets were flashing around me.

'Hetty, stop, stop, get on the floor!' my mother yelled.

I heard her cries above the din and threw myself on the

floor, but before I landed I saw the sick woman in the dormitory coming out of her bed and running towards us. A bullet hit her and, as if in a dream, I saw her crumple to the floor with blood streaming from her wounds.

'She got hit, she got hit!' I crawled towards my mother, sobbing.

She was rushed off to the sickbay, but died that night. She was the first death in our barrack. I stayed close to my mother for the rest of the day, and when we went to bed that evening I found two bullets in my bed. One of them had made a large hole in my book.

Small groups of people began to arrive at Belsen: gypsies from Hungary and Jewish families from Italy. Barracks were needed to house them. Trucks arrived with dismantled barracks from other camps in Germany. The men from our camp were ordered to erect the barracks, but few had skills in manual labour, so they went up very slowly. The barracks were erected on parts of the Appelplatz and to speed matters up, the SS brought in prisoners from the camp annexed to ours.

It was the first time that we had seen these poor creatures up close. They were dressed in white-and-grey cotton cloth, the uniform of the concentration camp. They would march into our camp early in the morning. The kapo (overseer) would scream when they passed through the gate, 'Hats off, face right,' in a salute to the SS Scharführer, who counted them as they came through. When their hats came off they revealed their shorn heads. They looked skinny and drawn. The kapo always screamed his orders, and how quickly those men moved! They lifted and carried and hammered the barracks together. They were from Eastern Europe, and I thought they spoke Polish or Estonian, but I couldn't understand them. I remember the smile one of the prisoners gave me though. His drawn face came alive, as if he wanted to tell me, 'I have not given up yet.'

Our barrack had become very crowded. Jacky's bed was claimed, so I had to share my bed with him. Luckily I wasn't a tall girl, so we slept head to tail, and we moved our suitcases to Mum's foot end.

We only saw Dad at lunchtime and for about an hour after he was finished at night. I used to wait near the gate for him and when he arrived deathly tired, often he would say to me, 'I can't go on any longer. How long before we are free again? Why is it all taking so long?'

I would take my father's hand, my heart bleeding to see him so depressed. 'Come on, Dad, you can do it. Don't lose hope. I'm sure it won't be long now.'

Later Dad and the boys would meet Mum near the gate. She went to work dressed in long leather boots she had brought from Holland. In these boots, covered by trousers, she would hide small pieces of carrots and smuggle them through the gates back to our camp. She risked her life twice each time she did that: first, by putting food in her boots in the peel kitchen, and second, by marching through the gates with it under the watchful eyes of the SS.

The food given to us became worse and worse. At noon we would get four centimetres of dry, hard bread. The barrack elder would cut up the square loaves of bread with a ruler while a group of people watched her like hawks to make sure no one got a fraction more. Sometimes we would get a square piece of butter or a spoonful of jam, but most of the time it was only bread. We also got soup — coloured water with parsnip or a piece of carrot floating in it. We were all terribly hungry and became masters at dividing our food rations so they would last for twenty-four hours.

One day Mum said to me, 'Hetty, if things don't get better soon, we will lose Dad.'

I nodded agreement.

'Would it be possible, Hetty,' Mum continued, 'for you and I to share one bowl of soup so Dad can have two?'

For a moment I considered the proposal and then agreed. Mum hugged me and said she would bring me some carrots every day. She could eat raw carrots in the peel kitchen.

'Hetty, the barrack elder wants to see you.' An elderly man standing near my bed delivered the message.

'What for?' I asked.

'You'd better come quickly to the dining room,' the man said as he walked away.

I climbed down from my bed and went to the dining room. The barrack elder beckoned me to come near.

'I want you to clear out your cupboard straightaway,' she said.

'We need the cupboard,' I objected.

'Do as you're told. I've given the cupboard to Mrs X,' she insisted.

A wave of disgust swept through me. Mrs X was one of a group of people who competed for favours from the barrack elder.

I got the key to the padlock and cleared the cupboard of our meagre belongings: our rations for the day, a few containers of vitamin tablets, calcium tablets, some pans, our soup bowls, spoons and forks, a few tea towels and our toothbrushes. We dumped everything on top of the bed. I hid the bread rations in one of the suitcases, out of view. I told Max and Jacky to keep watch over our goods while I collected our washing from the lines.

When I returned, the bed was deserted and Max and Jacky were nowhere in sight. A woman came over and told me what had happened. Apparently my father had come home early from work and the boys told him about the confiscated cupboard. My father was furious. He had stormed into the dining room and taken the barrack elder to task, voicing his disapproval in no uncertain terms. The barrack elder complained about my father to Albela, the camp elder, who summoned Dad to his office. Albela told my father that he was no longer allowed to enter our barrack and that he would lose two days' rations. This was the last straw for my father. He grabbed Albela by his necktie, and just as he was about to punch him, Scharführer Lubbe entered the office.

'What's going on?' Lubbe shouted. 'Lock up the criminal!'

Four strong men took hold of my father and dragged him across the Appelplatz to the small bunker.

While this was happening in Albela's office, I was waiting in the barrack for my father and brothers to return. Suddenly there was a knock on the window next to our beds. It was the same old man who had told me to see the barrack elder. He seemed very agitated and short of breath, and motioned for me to open the window.

'Your father had a fight with Albela and now they've put him in the bunker,' he gasped.

'Oh God, what will happen to him?' I started to cry.

The man tried to comfort me. 'Ask Mr Weiss. I'm sure he'll help as much as he can,' he said.

I nodded. Joseph Weiss was a wise man respected by everybody in our camp. 'I'd better get to the gate and meet my mother. I don't want her to hear it from someone else.'

I met Mum at the gate with Max and Jacky. 'Where's your father? Hasn't he come back from work yet?'

I started to say something, but was lost for words.

Mum became alarmed. 'What's the matter, Hetty? What's wrong?'

I blurted out the whole miserable story, while horror and shock registered on my mother's face.

'Let's go to the barrack, it's getting cold,' she said, after she'd recovered. 'Then I'll go to Mr Weiss to find out what happened and see if we can get some blankets and food to the bunker for Dad.'

Mum tidied herself up, then left with Max to find Mr Weiss.

They returned an hour later. 'Hetty! Quick! Give me two blankets and a pillow. I have to get them to Mr Weiss as soon as possible,' Mum said. 'The curfew starts at eight. I'll be back soon, and while I'm gone, make room for Max. He'll sleep with us tonight.'

'Wait, Mum, take a bread ration for Dad,' I said. I quickly opened the suitcase containing our rations and handed it to her. Then she was on her way with Max.

It was only minutes to eight when Mum and Max returned, and although Mum was near exhaustion I could see that she felt a little more at ease.

The four of us sat on top of the bed as Mum relayed what had happened. Mr Weiss had told her the offence Dad had committed in attacking Albela as camp elder had been taken very seriously by the SS and this was punishable by being sent away to a far worse concentration camp. However, Albela and Mr Weiss had persuaded Scharführer Lubbe that Dad would be suitably punished. Lubbe had agreed, but said he would also consider some additional punishment.

That night Mum and I could not sleep, not only as a result of the cramped conditions caused by Max sleeping with us, but also because our thoughts were constantly with Dad. The wind was howling through the camp and it was very cold. I prayed that Dad would be okay and I was happy that he had some of our blankets.

Mum and I talked softly. 'Tomorrow I'll go and see Lubbe,' she said.

'Why Mum? It's too dangerous — please don't!' I said. 'Think about it and wait and see what happens tomorrow. Try to get some sleep, you have to be up at three o'clock.'

I watched my mother's face: her eyelids were transparent blue-white, her face had become small and her skin showed a very white contrast to her jet-black hair. Despite all this, she was still my pretty mother. Her breathing became deeper, telling me that she was asleep. I carefully bent over and gently kissed her cheek, which felt hollow under my lips.

'Dear God,' I prayed, 'help us so all this will be over soon.' I turned on my side. Someone was snoring and sleep would not come. I stared at the outline of the sleepers in the dormitory as the hours went by slowly.

Herman's watch, which had never left my wrist since he was sent to Auschwitz, showed three o'clock. Gently, I woke Mum and told her that she had to go to work. She was so tired. She dressed herself on top of the blanket and put on her boots after she climbed down from the bed.

'I'll see if I can get back at lunchtime,' she whispered.

Mum had made up her mind. It has been said that a yiddishe mother will fight to the death for her family, and here I had the living proof. With no regard for her own safety, she would go and plead for her man.

'Look after the boys,' Mum said. She pulled my head down and kissed me. 'I'm running late. Try to get some sleep.' Then she left.

Oh, how I loved my mother.

I must have finally fallen asleep, as I woke up to the sound of rollcall. I quickly put on my clothes, and called Max and Jacky over. 'Come on, we must get to the Appelplatz,' I urged.

When we arrived, the people from our barrack were lined up only five metres away from the bunker where Dad was. I had never given the bunker a second glance before, but it was different now Dad was inside. It was a square, brick building about two metres by four metres, with a heavy padlocked door. There was a window, nailed up with a thick piece of plywood. The SS had not arrived yet, so I had an opportunity to get close to the wall without arousing suspicion.

'Dad,' I called softly, 'are you all right?'

I heard my father's voice. 'Is that you, Hetty?'

'Yes,' I said. 'Are you okay?'

'I'm okay,' Dad said. 'There's not much light. They blocked the window up.'

'I can see that,' I answered. 'Are you warm enough? It was so cold last night.'

'Don't worry. I'm warm enough.'

I could hear the barrack leaders calling the people to line up.

'I have to go now, Dad. I'll come back later.'

The SS were at it again. They had counted us three times already and made out that two people were missing. They screamed that we were not standing in line correctly and indiscriminately hit out at the unfortunate person in front of them. How could people go missing? There was no way out. There were guards everywhere.

As we resigned ourselves to being at rollcall for a long time, a small party of men approached. Lubbe, the Scharführer in charge of rollcall, Albela and two of his lieutenants walked past us towards the bunker. My heart was pounding. What was in store for Dad? The bunker door was opened and my father was ordered outside. I strained to see what was happening through the crowd, but could only hear the loud voice of Lubbe as he addressed my father. I felt helpless. What could I do?

Then we heard the door of the bunker being shut and the party went back in the direction of Albela's office.

It took more than three hours that morning before Albela blew the whistle marking the end of rollcall. Usually after rollcall I would return to the barrack immediately, but this time I was in no hurry. Max also stayed behind. Together we walked slowly towards the bunker. With about a metre to go, we stopped. Max turned towards me and, making out that he was speaking to me, he called out to Dad in the bunker. Dad answered immediately. Max asked what had happened when Lubbe and Albela came to the bunker during rollcall.

'Lubbe told me to apologise to Albela, and after I did he gave me two whacks about the head,' Dad said.

'Are you all right, Dad?' Max asked.

'Yes, I'm okay. Don't worry. Can you get me something to eat, Hetty? She is with you, isn't she, Max?' Dad asked.

'Yes, Dad,' I said. 'I'll ask Mr Weiss to bring you one of our food rations and something to drink.'

'Okay,' Dad said. 'See what you can do.'

Max and I left for the barrack. I collected our daily ration from the barrack elder. She gave me only four rations; for two days Dad would get nothing. No words were needed. One ration would go immediately to Dad, and the four of us would share the other three.

At about one o'clock Mum came back as she had intended. We told her what had happened at the Appelplatz that morning and assured her that Dad was okay.

'I know,' she said. 'I went to speak to him before coming to the barrack. But now I must go to see Lubbe.'

'I'll go with you, Mum,' I said.

At first Mum refused, but when she saw my determination, she agreed. We arrived at the Appelplatz at the same moment as the last work detail was marching off. Lubbe was in conversation with Albela. He seemed to be in one of his good moods.

'Wish me good luck,' Mum said, and squeezed my hand.

She started to walk slowly towards Albela and Lubbe. At a respectful distance she stopped and waited. Albela spotted her first and spoke to my mother. How courageous she looks, I thought. Her head was lifted, to look up to the towering SS man. After about two minutes the conversation was over and I saw Mum coming back towards me.

'Let's go to the boys,' she said, smiling.

On the way to the barrack, she told me what she had said to Lubbe. She had addressed him as 'Hauptsturmführer', knowing quite well that Lubbe was only a Scharführer. She had flattered his ego this way. She had apologised to him in broken German for what my father had done, and portrayed him as a worried parent. His children were without supervision every day of the week, as she was always working and therefore could not attend to them at all. It seemed that Lubbe could understand this, and he told her that children needed discipline. He said that the matter had already been reported to Berlin, but that he would give it some thought.

Although we could not be sure that Dad would not be sent away, we had some hope that Mum's appeal would work. That afternoon, the court gave my father four days' bunker time, which meant that in two days he could come out again. We all went to bed early that night. The emotional pressure had worn us out completely.

More and more people started to arrive in Belsen. The Hungarian camp next to ours was now empty — the SS had transported the inhabitants away. It was joined with the Häftling camp. The men in this camp had their hair shorn and wore grey-and-white pyjamas. Some of them had no shoes.

The weather got even colder and it rained sometimes, which turned the Appelplatz and roads into quagmires. The SS let us stand for hours at rollcall, and from our position we could observe that the prisoners in the Häftlinge camp experienced a worse fate. Sometimes, long after we were allowed to go back to the barracks, those poor creatures were still standing at rollcall. Their faces were grey, their cheeks hollow, their eyes deep in their sockets, and some of them had the look of cornered animals.

After thirteen long weeks in Belsen the appalling food started taking its toll. Tall men were the first to die from hunger. During a rollcall early in February, Scharführer Rau selected two young men to take charge of the small crematorium at the far end of the camp.

In the beginning there was not much work for the crematorium, but now it worked day and night, as day by day more and more people died.

Dysentery was rife in the camp and at night the people who had to go to the toilets kept us awake. Sometimes a person did not make it in time, and the vile stench penetrated the nose even during sleep. Our family was lucky; none of us had dysentery. Could it have been something to do with our constitutions or was it the good food we had eaten before we were interned? I remember the beautiful juicy brisket my grandmother used to cook for us, which Opa brought home from the abattoirs. I could see it: Opa cutting the meat with a very sharp, long knife into even, thick slices. He would serve each one of us a generous portion before he served himself. He always started his meal with the meat, which he meticulously cut into small square pieces and then topped with a small square piece of juicy fat, relishing every bite. He taught me to eat the juicy fat as he said that it was good for my bones and brain. When he finished with the meat, Oma handed him a fresh plate, fork and knife for his vegetables.

As I sat on my bed in Belsen I saw my grandparents' living room in front of me and recalled the happy faces around the table. I saw the spread of food and my Oma's happy smile, and my heart was crying that this was gone forever.

Hygiene had deteriorated to a standard that cannot be comprehended: no soap, no water. I had been wearing the same clothes for months. I decided to change at least my jumper. When I pulled the jumper over my head, it turned inside out. My eyes fell on something crawling — lice! My armpits were putrid with nits. I started to kill them between my thumbnails but it was useless. I looked in the suitcase to see if I could find another jumper. I put the offensive jumper in the suitcase hoping the lice would die. I did not tell a soul, I was so ashamed. Mum had been very careful about keeping our heads free of lice, and here they were, under my arms.

Chapter 4

At the end of May 1944, a new transport of people arrived from Westerbork. The group was made up of diamond merchants. Barracks had been erected for them near the hospital barrack. The diamond people were given special privileges. They did not have to join work details and were given double food rations. The weather had improved again, and during the day you could see these diamond people sunning themselves near the clothes line or just strolling through the camp all nicely dressed.

Dad told us that he was going to Albela's office to try to get his name on the list with the diamond group. Dad had been a skilled diamond tradesman before he moved into textiles. My father's youngest brother, Max, and his wife, Clara, had come with us to Belsen in the same transport. Max, too, was skilled with diamonds. Before Dad went to Albela's office, he discussed the situation with Uncle Max. They both agreed to give it a go; the prospect of not going to work at six o'clock in the morning was worth a try.

After a few days Dad told us that all our names had been

registered with the diamond group. However, things did not turn out as we hoped. Dad and Uncle Max still had to go to work every morning and they did not receive double food rations.

Mum's talk with Lubbe when Dad was in the bunker had a pleasant result. From the end of May, the women who worked in the kitchen were allowed half a day a week off so they could look after their families. How happy we were to have Mum with us for a half a day. Mum and I attended to tasks such as washing our only sheets. We had long run out of the soap we'd brought from Holland, so we soaked our washing in salt. When our washing was on the line, I would sit nearby to keep watch so it would not be stolen.

Only three other garments hung on the line: a bra, a singlet and a pair of panties that showed stains of menstruation. Strange, I thought: most of the women had stopped menstruating shortly after arriving in Belsen. I never got my period any more and neither did Mum. Maybe it was not such a bad thing. After all, how in the world could we have managed without pads or soap to keep us clean? I had no idea how it could be achieved and deeply pitied the woman who had to cope with this problem.

It was peaceful under the clothes lines. I looked at the blue sky and saw a small white cloud. I looked at the shimmering distance of the Lüneburg Heath, and as my gaze travelled through the wire fences, I saw a bird high in the sky and felt a deep yearning to be free again. The pain of being enclosed was nearly unbearable.

One day, the camp grapevine let us know that high-ranking SS from Berlin were to visit us. The whole camp received a spring clean. We were shown how our beds had to be made up each morning — smooth and flat at the top, and not a ripple was to show in the blankets. We were not allowed to store or hide anything in our beds. For those who had a cupboard that wasn't hard, but our family had problems. Our suitcases with our belongings were stored on the end of Mum's bed, where they had been under our constant surveillance. Now we had to put them under the bunk. I packed all our clothing in one suitcase, and another one with our soup bowls and other belongings. The barrack was scrubbed and cleaned from top to bottom. Those who did not go to work had to do the cleaning.

Our food miraculously began to improve. With our bread rations, we received a small square of butter, and a packet of Limburger cheese for the week. The cheese smelt terrible. We had never eaten it at home, but the fact that it was made in Holland somehow made me feel that we had not been forgotten. Amazing how this small packet of cheese seemed to give me comfort. Our midday soup also improved. It was thicker and even pieces of meat and potatoes could be found in it.

We became cunning. We waited to collect our soup until

the large forty-litre container that held the mixture was two-thirds empty, as at the bottom the soup was thicker. We had our midday soup with Dad in the dining room. He had been allowed back into our barrack after apologising to the barrack elder. How happy we were if we discovered a piece of meat in our soup!

One day, I received what I thought was a very large piece of meat. Excitedly, I returned with the bowl to the table. Dad lifted the large piece from the bowl with a fork so he could divide it between us. We were horrified to see that it was not meat, but a filthy cleaning cloth, which had been cooked with our soup. What should we do, we pondered. How could we eat this soup? How unhygienic! But the worst thing was that the volume of the soup left in the bowl had dropped considerably after removal of the cloth. I decided to take it back. I put the cloth in the bowl and showed the barrack elder. She just removed the cloth and topped up the bowl with more soup.

'Don't worry,' she said. 'It won't kill you!'

I gave Dad half the contents of my bowl as I had promised Mum. Our eyes met across the table and we knew what the other was thinking. To stay alive, we had to eat the soup. Our hunger had reduced us to this. I picked up my spoon and started to eat.

It was about the middle of June when our barrack was inspected. The inspection took place while we were at rollcall. When we returned, the barrack elder informed us that everything was okay. We were relieved, and within a few days the barrack looked a mess again and our cases were back on Mum's bed.

My Uncle Max had always been my favourite uncle. We didn't see much of him as he was working in the kitchen, sometimes for eighteen hours at a time. They were well fed, those lucky kitchen workers. Clara worked with Mum in the peel kitchen, but she didn't need to eat the raw carrots as Uncle Max stole plenty of food.

The days when Uncle Max was free and Clara came home from work they would have 'dinner' on top of Clara's bunk. They hooked a blanket to the rafters to give themselves privacy. From our bed we used to see them going behind their blankets, and we knew that they were eating and that they would not be so hungry. But they never offered any food to us. This is how it was in Belsen. People became very mean, only thinking of their own survival. It had become obvious that Uncle Max and Clara were avoiding us, scared that we would ask them for food. Max and Jacky complained bitterly about it, but Mum forbade them to go begging. They were still so young and could not understand how their uncle had changed.

Thousands and thousands of old shoes were brought in to the camp by truck and unloaded into a mountain. My father was chosen for a new work detail: the shoe brigade. The work itself was not heavy, but very dirty. The workers had to separate the top leather from the soles with a sharp knife. Among the two hundred workers were academics, businessmen, rabbis and engineers. To break the monotony of this mind-deadening work, they gave lectures on various subjects while they were working.

In July the weather was lovely and an optimistic feeling swept through our camp. We received some news of the outside world when new transports arrived from Westerbork. How totally isolated we were. Did people in Holland or anyone else in the rest of the world still remember us? Other nationalities would at times get a food parcel from the Red Cross, but those of us who came from Holland never received anything.

Max's twelfth birthday was on 22 July. For days he'd been nagging Mum for permission to see Uncle Max on his birthday to ask for something to eat. At first Mum refused but then gave in.

'How can I deprive my child of a chance to get something to eat?' she said.

Although my hunger was as great as Max's and everyone else's, I could not agree. The thought of going to ask my once-favourite uncle for something he apparently wasn't willing to give voluntarily went against every fibre of my being. I would not reduce myself to begging for food yet.

Mum had managed to be free on the day of Max's birthday. During the lunchbreak, Max went over to Clara's bed, where Uncle Max was sleeping. Hesitantly he called out. We were watching from a distance and saw the blanket being lifted and Uncle Max's head appear. After a few words, Max was invited up and disappeared behind the blanket. He remained there about ten minutes and when he climbed down again, he had in his hand a thick slice of white bread with butter and sugar. His face was shining with happiness. When he returned to our bed, he handed his present to Mum, offering to share it between us. Mum cut off a small piece for Jacky, and after my refusal of a share, she told Max to eat the lot as it was his birthday. With small bites, he relished this unexpected delicacy.

Perhaps Uncle Max's conscience was bothering him, because the next day at lunchtime he called Max over to Clara's bed. When Max returned, there were two more slices of bread with butter and sugar for 'Hetty and Jacky'. I divided them between the five of us, keeping Mum's share until she returned from work that night. How good it tasted when I sank my teeth into this heavenly windfall! I am sure the finest cake could not have surpassed it.

We did not receive any more handouts from Uncle Max.

It was August 1944 and so hot that it was impossible to sleep. It was better outside the barrack than in, so we spent most of our time outside. Sitting outside could be done in comfort if a chair could be found, otherwise you just sat on the dusty, dry ground. There was not a green leaf in sight. Grass did not grow and everything was covered in a dreary grey dust.

Despite the heat, we still had to attend agonising hours of rollcall. One day the SS left us standing there for eight hours. We had supposedly not cleaned our barrack properly and Scharführer Red Müller, the officer in charge, was in a foul mood. He would storm into the barrack and scream like a maniac, pulling the blankets off beds that were not made up to standard. He would open the cupboards, and if he found bowls with any soup still left in them, which the owner had saved to eat later, he would throw them through the barrack, shouting at the top of his voice. It was his usual practice to hold onto our bread rations for a day or two after such a performance. We had gone hungry for so long now that we got used to it. We became lethargic and our speech slowed down. People were dying every day.

Red Müller was a bully who delighted in screaming at the elderly people. These poor people, with fright showing on their faces and their legs trembling, knew his fury would be turned on them. He would hit them with his fist and punish them by making them stand for many hours at the gate with their caps in their hands in wind, rain or in the burning sun. He also confiscated their rations for two or sometimes four days. Müller was a sadistic monster.

Our food did not arrive on time any more. The kitchen worked day and night to deal with the influx of people to Belsen. The carriers could not cope and sometimes our soup containers would not arrive until eight o'clock at night. We were waiting for this little bit of soup. The warm, inferior concoction would somehow sustain us for a while.

Dad heard through the camp grapevine that Uncle Max was in the bunker — not the small bunker Dad had been kept in, but at the camp section for the SS.

'What happened?' I asked.

'I'm not sure,' Dad said, 'but I've been told that he stole a kilogram of butter and they caught him.'

What would happen to my uncle? I knew how cruel and vicious the SS were. The next two days were unbearable with no news, but on the third day, late in the afternoon, I saw Uncle Max enter our barrack. He looked pale. Dad was resting on Mum's bed when I informed him that Uncle Max had returned. He immediately went over to find out what had happened.

Both of them returned to our beds. Close up, Uncle Max looked terrible. Our eyes met and despite my resentment, I threw my arms around his neck and kissed him. I was really happy to see him again. For a moment, the old Uncle Max emerged. His eyes smiled as he told me that I had grown. He then told us that he indeed was caught with a kilogram of butter, which he had tried to smuggle into our camp. For two days he had been held in solitary confinement, with the SS coming in every couple of hours to give him a beating. It was his strong physique that had carried him through and he was lucky he wasn't sent to Auschwitz. He was very tired, as he'd had no food for two days.

'Better go and lie down and get some rest before Clara comes back from work. You need it,' Dad said.

Uncle Max agreed. He patted my head and walked toward Clara's bed. With some difficulty, he climbed on top and we saw him disappear behind the blanket. It was good that the family ties were restored, and when I went to sleep that night I thanked God that Uncle Max had been spared and that he had become one of our family again. The next day, he was allocated to the shoe brigade as he was not allowed to return to the kitchen.

The heat was oppressive. The air in the barrack was stifling. No one could sleep at night. The water supply was cut off for long periods, so when the taps were running there was a tremendous rush as everyone wanted to fill up bottles or buckets. Some lucky ones were able to give themselves a quick wash.

The deliberate rationing of the water and the chaotic result of this amused the SS tremendously. They smiled and watched the human misery from a distance. The heat also affected our sewerage system, which was not constructed to cater for so many people.

During this heatwave, one evening Mum told me to come with her to the washhouse. Her face told me there was something terribly wrong. When we entered the washhouse, I saw my father standing in the only pair of pants he possessed, covered in excrement from his shoes to his armpits. His face was also not too clean.

'What happened?' I gasped.

Dad told me that Red Müller had come to the shoe workplace and demanded four men to clean out the latrines — to humiliate him Chief Rabbi Dasberg was chosen first, next were my father and Uncle Max, and the fourth was a man named Myer.

'Was the Rabbi standing in the pit?' I asked.

'No,' Dad said. 'We wouldn't let him do that. We handed the buckets up to him to cart away. Of course he got dirty, but we did not let him stand in the latrine pit.'

'All right, get those filthy clothes off,' Mum told Dad.

Luckily, the washhouse was empty. I discreetly turned my back to my father while he undressed. In the meantime, I filled the trough with water. It was a wonder that the water was on. Mum handed me Dad's pants. Phew! What a smell! What a mess! Quickly, I dumped the pants in the water, which at once turned into a miniature latrine. I let the dirty water run out and repeated the process again and again. Dad's underwear and shirt got the same treatment. To no avail. I couldn't get those pants clean again. There was no soap or detergent to help me. I asked Mum to give me the scrubbing brush, but this wasn't successful either. While Dad washed himself, Mum tried to clean his shoes.

In the middle of our misery, I couldn't help but laugh when I saw Dad in his clean clothing. Mum had borrowed a pair of pants for Dad from someone, but they were far too short. Mum and I discussed various ways of getting his pants clean again. Throwing them away was unthinkable. Clothing was impossible to find in Belsen, so we needed to hang on to what we had. We decided to let the pants, shirt and underwear soak overnight in the water, and I would make another attempt to clean the pants in the morning. Of one thing we could be sure: no one would steal them.

The next day after rollcall, I went back to the washhouse and rinsed the clothes again and again for about an hour. The shirt and underwear, although stained, were reasonably clean, but remained smelly. I decided to leave the pants soaking for another day, but took the shirt and underwear to the lines to dry.

For two more days I soaked, rinsed and scrubbed the pants, and when at long last I hung them out to dry, I could still smell the latrine. I hoped that the sun and air would take care of that problem.

Despite their poor appearance, Dad was grateful when I handed him the pants that night, so he could return the borrowed pair he had been wearing. I hoped that Dad would never have to clean a latrine again. I didn't think I could cope a second time.

Chapter 5

It was September 1944 and the hot days were finally over. The weather was beautiful. Every day transports would arrive in our camp. The dining room disappeared, and beds were placed in the area. A small corner stayed reserved for the barrack elder, and a long trestle table served as a counter from which we collected our daily rations.

During the first weeks in September, a small transport of women arrived from Westerbork and among them was Sonja. The reunion with Sonja was a high point in our dreary lives, and at the same time a sorrow, since we'd thought she was safe in Amsterdam. She told us that she had met my mother's brother and his family in Westerbork and, very sadly, they had been sent with the last transport to Auschwitz a few weeks ago.

My mother was devastated. She asked Sonja all sorts of questions. What happened? They had been hiding in a farm in Drenthe for three years. They were so safe there! How did they get caught? Sonja did not know the answers. We were very sad to hear this news. After Mum had a good cry, she said that perhaps they would be all right. We were not so sure, but we did not tell Mum this.

The conversation continued about old friends and relatives, when the sunlight caught the ring on Sonja's hand.

'That's a lovely ring.' Mum said. When Sonja stretched out her hand, Mum recognised it at once. 'It's mine!'

'That's right,' Sonja said. 'I found it between the towels in your linen cupboard after the SS took you away, but you should have it back.'

Mum's face lit up. This ring reminded her of happier times, when everything was normal in our lives. It was a precious memory of a wedding anniversary with the whole family present. She slipped the ring on, but it was too big: Mum, like everyone else, had lost a lot of weight. She rolled it in a handkerchief and put it in her bra. The safest place to keep anything in the camp was on your body.

The lovely weather continued and on the days Mum didn't have to work we would sit around the tables outside the barrack.

Elderly women and some old men sat around chatting with each other. They talked about the latest death of friends and relatives. They talked about the war, sickness and, above all, food. They would talk about cakes with fresh cream, juicy steaks and all the delicacies which took their fancy. And in our imagination, we could see, yes, even smell, the aromas of the food they described.

One morning I was looking in the mirror that had been presented to me in Westerbork, while I was combing my hair. Since my mother had cut it in the train the night we were picked up, it had grown back to a beautiful length again. I smiled at myself in the mirror and noticed that a small hole had appeared in one of my front teeth. I decided to go and see the dentist. A small medical centre was set up near Albela's office. You could see a dentist there during certain hours. The medical centre was initially set up for the SS but at times the dentist was allowed to attend to us. I went there after rollcall, and was told by the nurse to come back after three o'clock that afternoon. When I returned two people were there before me, so I had to wait. When my turn came, the nurse called me in. I entered the room and was met by a gentle man of about sixty. The room was completely fitted out as a first-class dental surgery. Everything was clean and shiny and the dentist wore a spotless white coat. I imagined I was back home. After he had seated me in the dental chair, the dentist asked me what the problem was.

'I have a hole in my front tooth,' I said.

'Let's have a look, young lady. Open your mouth.'

'Well,' he said after examining my teeth, 'you also have large holes in two of your molars. We shall soon fix them.'

He started drilling my molars. No anaesthetic was given. I grabbed hold of the arms of my chair so I could withstand the pain. While he was drilling away, he told me he would fill the holes in my molars with white cement.

'This way,' he said, 'we can preserve them until we are home again.'

When he finished the molars he started on my front tooth, and applied a temporary filling. By the time that was finished, I had been in the chair for more than two hours and was glad it was over. I was told to come back in a week's time.

When I left the surgery, it was starting to get dark. The camp was deserted. I walked quickly towards our barrack. When I arrived, the family was seated on top of our beds. We were lucky to have top bunks. At least we had somewhere to sit. Sometimes there was a lot of bickering in the barracks between the people in the lower beds and those above them. The space between the bunks did not allow the person on the lower bunk to sit upright. This created jealousy, and at times many angry words could be heard when the person at the top climbed up or down.

I returned to the dentist a week later.

'Oh, there you are,' the dentist said when I entered the surgery, 'I've been waiting especially for you. I'm not too well and as soon as I'm finished with you I'll lie down.'

I sat in the chair and the dentist quickly started to remove the temporary filling from my front tooth. When he completed the removal and prepared the tooth for its permanent filling, he instructed the nurse to prepare a mixture of ceramic glazing. The nurse did not respond.

'Why are you not doing what I told you to do?' he asked.

'The ceramic glazing is only for the SS. They'll notice if you use some of it,' she answered.

'Do what you're told and be quick about it before the rest of the filling sets.' The dentist spoke softly but urgently.

Reluctantly, the nurse prepared the mixture and the dentist finished my front tooth expertly.

'Here, Hetty,' he said, 'look at yourself.'

He gave me the mirror. He had done a beautiful job. My teeth reflected in the mirror like white pearls.

'Now,' the dentist said, 'look after them as best you can. You're a very pretty girl. I couldn't put white cement in your front tooth. It would be a shame. Go back to your barrack and remember, no drinking or eating for four hours. Oh, I feel tired,' he finished.

'Are you all right, sir?' I asked. He looked quite ill.

'Yes. But I think I'll go and lie down after you go.'

The next day, the news that the dentist had died in his sleep went through the camp. I was very upset by his passing. He really meant it when he said to me, 'I have been waiting for you,' and now I knew why he had not been concerned about the consequences of stealing white ceramic glazing for my tooth from the SS. He had known I would be his last patient.

At four o'clock every day, the dead bodies were

collected for cremation. When the cart with the dentist's body passed through the gate, I was there to pay him my last respects. I walked as far as I could along the perimeter of our camp, parallel with the road leading to the crematorium. When I could go no further, I watched the cart disappear into the distance. My heart was crying. I remembered the dentist's kind eyes and gentle hands, his reassuring smile when sometimes he had to hurt me. 'Oh God, oh God,' I cried. He was a good man. He did not deserve to die yet or to have such an undignified end. My eyes were burning with tears as I slowly returned to the barrack.

In November 1944 a large tent was erected on the flat ground about fifty metres from our camp. Soon after, we saw long columns of women passing our camp. They were poorly dressed. Some had no shoes at all; their feet were covered only in dirty rags. Most wore scarves to hide their naked scalps. It was eerie to watch. They made no sound as they shuffled past. They were housed in the large tent with only bales of straw to sleep on.

Our men had been ordered to dig the latrines for the women. They were in the open, but the women had come to the point where they didn't care. I could observe all this with ease, as our barrack was very close to the dividing fence between our barrack and their tent. All the time we could hear them fighting and screaming among themselves. Sometimes a kapo with a whip would enter the tent and mete out a belting in order to restore some peace.

On the second day after their arrival, a group of the women came up to our dividing fence to talk. We soon found out that there were Dutch women among them. My father and mother went to the fence out of curiosity. After a while my mother came back to the barrack and found me sitting on top of the bed. I had no inclination to go near them. The sight of them walking silently past our camp the day before had scared me to the depths of my soul.

'Aunty Beth is there, and Sonja's mother,' Mum said. 'Dad's talking to them right now. I've come back to take some clothing to them, they have nothing. Look in the suitcase, Hetty, see if we can spare something.'

I pulled out a red cardigan belonging to Mum and a flannel pyjama top of Dad's.

'That's about all we have that will fit them,' I said.

I found the black woollen jumper I had packed away because of the lice.

'Do you think we could give them this jumper, Mum?' I asked. 'It's not very clean.'

'That's all right,' Mum said. 'They can change it for food if they don't want to keep it. Considering the state they're in, I suppose everything is welcome.'

Mum left in a hurry. As I slowly repacked our suitcase I

heard Eva from a bed further on, calling my name.

'Hetty, can I come over?'

'Of course,' I said.

Eva climbed onto our bed. Eva was a few years older than me. We had spoken briefly now and then in the barrack or at rollcall.

'I went to the fence with my mother, and those women told us that they had come from Auschwitz and that they were burning people there,' Eva said.

'What do you mean, burning people?' I asked.

'Well,' Eva said, 'they put them in an oven and burn them.'

'You're crazy,' I said. 'I don't believe it.'

But Eva was adamant. 'I'm not making it up,' she said. 'It's true!'

I sat motionless, trying to digest what she had told me. Many questions went through my head. How could the SS have done it? No one would willingly let themselves be put in an oven … of course, the picture I conjured up in my mind was of a kitchen stove. Eva was absolutely mad, I decided.

When Mum and Dad arrived back, I asked them straightaway, 'Is it true that they burned people in Auschwitz?'

Mum looked at Dad, unable to answer.

'Yes, Hetty,' Dad said.

'But how did they do it?' I asked.

'When the trains arrived in Auschwitz, mothers and children were separated from the fathers, and then they were taken to a building where they were told they had to take a bath,' Dad replied. 'They were all given a towel and a piece of soap, but instead of water, gas came out of the showers. They gassed our people first and then they burned them in huge crematoriums.'

I opened my mouth to say something but could not utter a word. A kaleidoscope of pictures went through my mind. I saw my lovely grandmother gasping for breath. I saw people rushing the doors and trying to open them. When at long last the horrible reality sank in I knew that never, never again would our lives be the same. I knew that there was no hope of ever seeing my grandparents again, nor many of our large family.

My mother was crying. She also knew there was no hope of ever seeing her parents again. Dad tried to comfort Mum as best as he could. His eyes were burning with tears. How hopeless we felt. What could we do?

I started to pray that God would give us strength, and asked him to help us get out of this inhuman situation. My tears were running freely. Mum recovered somewhat and stroked my hair to calm me down.

Long after the lights went out that night, you could hear people discussing the horrific news we had learned this evening. Like most of the people in our barrack, I did not sleep that night. Now I knew why I had not wanted to go to the fence to meet the women. I had sensed the evil spirits surrounding them as they shuffled past the day before. I had felt their pain and sorrow and now it scared me even more.

When Mum left at three o'clock I lay awake, staring into the darkness. How are we going to get out of this place? I wondered. Why is no one in this world helping us? I was glad when daylight broke.

Life in our camp became very, very crowded. More and more barracks had been built on the Appelplatz. They looked dark and forbidding. There were hardly any windows in them and they were a lighter construction. Inside, the three-tiered bunks were placed very close together so more people could be housed in them.

A storm blew away the big tent in which the women of Auschwitz were housed. In the wind and pouring rain those poor women stood without any protection against nature's brute force. They looked like white ghosts in the downpour. In the afternoon the shoe detail was sent back to our camp so the women could shelter in their workplace. A few days later the women were moved to another part of Belsen.

The shoe detail went back to work again. The weather was bleak and the drizzly rain made the hours standing on rollcall more and more trying. At least our feet were dry. Dad had smuggled out shoes for us under his heavy coat. They were made of heavy, oiled black leather and had wooden soles. They resembled Dutch clogs. Dad had taken an enormous risk in bringing them through the gate. Many men were caught as they passed through, which meant a beating and hours standing near the gate in rain and wind under the watchful eyes of the SS guards. Their food rations would be cancelled for days. Luckily, Dad had come through safely.

It was about the last week in November when Mum told us that for the next four weeks we could go to barrack twenty-six at four o'clock every day to drink a glass of milk. The sister of Frau Albela would give it to us. When I asked how that had come about, Mum told me that she had sold her diamond ring. She had also received twenty large potatoes, three jam jars of sugar and a jar of salt. She pulled a jar of sugar from our suitcase, shielding it with her body from prying eyes. Everybody was so hungry that if it was known that you had some extra food, it might be stolen, so you either ate it or exchanged it for something else. We had not seen sugar for more than a year. Mum opened the jar and gave Jacky, then Max and me a teaspoonful. I relished the sweetness as it slowly dissolved in my mouth.

'Every day you'll get a spoonful of sugar to keep up your strength,' Mum said.

She then showed us the enormous potatoes, which she had hidden between our clothes in our suitcase. But what could you do with raw potatoes? I took a knife and cut a big chunk from one of them. But it was horrible and even with all my hunger I could not eat it. What could we do with these potatoes if we could not cook them?

Mum closed the suitcase firmly and said, 'From now on, one of us must always guard the suitcase. Our bed must not be left alone at any time. You organise the schedule, Hetty, so you can each take your turn.'

How happy we were. We felt like millionaires, and when Dad came home from work he was shown our treasures. Mum gave Dad a spoonful of sugar, but he said that the sugar should be kept for us children.

Terrible things were happening in our camp. In the past few days, people from other barracks were told to move out with all their belongings to other barracks. The order usually came when the work details had just returned late in the afternoon and everybody was very tired. The moves lasted until late into the night and this soul-destroying task had to be done without lights. The people were in a panic to find beds in the allocated barracks — those recently completed, ominous-looking barracks near the Appelplatz. As the beds were so close together, people pushed and struggled to find a bed in the dark, only to discover that there were no mattresses, or planks underneath to carry a mattress. It was bedlam. Our barrack had until now escaped the ruckus, but we knew our turn would come eventually.

One Friday night, a cold and drizzly rain was falling

when someone came into the barrack and urgently requested able men to help at the barrack for the old people who had been ordered to move.

When our group had arrived in February two barracks had been reserved for the old and the sick. The SS were very scared of infectious diseases as they could carry to their quarters. A fence surrounded both barracks. We were not allowed to come close to it. When someone got seriously sick they were taken to the hospital. They seldom returned. Daily you could see bodies being taken on the lonely journey to the crematorium.

Dad told us about the appalling conditions of the newly designated barrack for the old and the sick. It was the same story as before — not enough mattresses. They had to leave some very frightened and exhausted old people lying on the cold floor. We were very depressed when we heard this sad story, but out of something bad came something good — for us, at least. In the old people's barrack, stoves were burning to give some warmth. Dad had made arrangements with a nurse to cook some of our potatoes. The price was five large potatoes for the cook.

Chapter 6

The next day, 1 December 1944, we had to move to another barrack. Everyone packed their meagre belongings together, and slowly the barrack in which we had lived for ten months emptied. It was very unsettling. The barrack had become our home, our beds so familiar. We had slept, eaten and talked, sitting close together as a family unit. Now there was this uncertainty again, that feeling we had experienced so many times at home in Amsterdam when the SS had gone from door to door to bring people out of their houses. We had heard the knocks on other doors and had always been relieved when the sound of heavy boots passed our home without stopping. Here in Belsen it was no different. Uprooting people en masse was a cunning and sadistic technique that created panic in our hearts.

Mum, Dad, Jacky and Max had gone to investigate the new barrack and to find us a bed. I was left behind to guard the suitcases and our blankets, rolled up in a bundle. While I was sitting on top of our bed, I surveyed the near-empty barrack. Here and there some discarded or forgotten possessions were lying around. They won't be there for long, I thought. Someone will have a use for them.

Mum and Dad arrived back after about two hours.

'What took you so long?' I asked.

'I have a surprise for you,' Mum said.

They climbed up and Mum opened a bundle wrapped in some old cloth.

'Here, you may eat it all,' she said, as she handed me one of the large potatoes cooked in its skin and still boiling hot.

'How did you do this?' I asked.

'Well,' Dad answered, 'it was really your mother's idea to take advantage of the chaos in our camp at the moment. We went to the hospital with the potatoes, and, as everyone was moving around with bundles and suitcases, no one noticed anything.'

While the potatoes were being cooked in the hospital, they had gone to find beds in the new barrack. They had also found two mattresses, and they had to find some planks for underneath as well. Max and Jacky had stayed behind to guard the beds. Mum and Dad had returned to the hospital to collect the potatoes.

While Mum and Dad were telling me the story, I had peeled away the skin of half the potato and broken a piece away. I started to eat it slowly as it was still piping hot. I had only finished half the potato when I found I couldn't eat another bite. My stomach couldn't handle any more food, even though I would have sworn I could have eaten a whole cow, I was so hungry when I started.

I looked up at Mum in surprise. 'I can't eat any more.'

'Go slowly,' Mum urged, 'your stomach has shrunk. Better keep the rest for breakfast.' She opened the cloth which still held two potatoes for Max and Jacky.

I put my half a potato with the other two, and Mum put them in the suitcase.

'Well,' she asked, 'was it good?'

Was it good? Of course it was good! For the first time in months my stomach was full.

'We'd better be going, it's getting late,' Dad said.

We climbed down from our bed for the last time. Dad took the two suitcases and Mum and I each carried a bundle of blankets.

It was dark when we left the barrack. The weather was mild. There were still a few people shuffling around but most were already in their barracks. We crossed the Appelplatz. When we arrived in our new barrack it was not as bad as I had imagined it would be. Some people were burning a candle. It gave them a dim light and helped us find our beds.

Max and Jacky were glad to see us as they had been a bit scared in the new surroundings. Mum gave them each a potato before we made up our bed. The sight of the potato soon stopped any complaints from the boys. But even before Max could finish his potato Dad told him they had to leave in time for the curfew.

Mum had managed to get a top bunk for the two of us again with Jacky on the bed below us. He had to share a bed with another woman as there was a shortage. Soon we were told that all the lights had to be out. The barrack was in total darkness. Mum had fallen asleep as soon as her head hit the pillow, but I could not sleep. I was staring into the darkness and listening to the sounds of so many people resting in an exhausted sleep. I turned on my side and looked through the window next to our bed. I could see the deserted Appelplatz dimly lit from the big light on the gate, the barracks throwing their shadow on the ground. I leant over the side of the bunk and as my eyes became accustomed to the dark, I could see Jacky sleeping peacefully on the bed below. I must have dozed, as I woke up when Mum gently untangled herself from the blanket to go to work. We had all gone to sleep fully dressed. Being in an unfamiliar place we felt safer with our clothes on.

Max came early in the morning and told us to give him our beakers so he could get some 'coffee' for Jacky and myself. It didn't take him long to return. He handed the beakers up to me, having difficulty not spilling the coffee, as our bed was much higher than in the previous barrack. Jacky and I snuggled under my blanket together. The closeness of our bodies radiated heat. It was lovely to feel warm. We sipped the drink while we observed our surroundings. In the light of the morning we did not see many familiar faces. To our surprise we noticed that men were also sleeping in the barrack. How that had come about we did not know, and we did not much care. Women were not prudish anymore, and dressed and undressed and washed themselves, in front of strangers. Who would want to look at those skinny women anyway? The one thought that drove everybody on was finding food to stay alive.

The three of us stayed in the barrack all day. We only left it to stand at rollcall. Before we went to the Appelplatz we had covered the suitcase containing our precious sugar with a blanket, making sure that our bed was made according to SS standards.

The hours went by slowly, as we waited for our parents' return. We didn't feel at home yet in this new barrack. It housed twice as many people as the previous one.

Max got us our soup at lunchtime and, as usual, we saved a bowl for Dad. He was always so hungry when he came home from work. When it was time, the boys went to meet him near the gate, then they all went back for Mum later. The hours Mum had to work had grown longer and longer. There were only two kitchens in the camp to cater for the tremendous influx of people in Belsen.

It had been a long, long day. I was so happy to see everyone again. They all climbed onto our bed. It was more difficult now as there was not much room to sit. Most of the other people also sat on their bunks, and when you climbed up or down you could unintentionally step on the person below.

The next day was the same routine. At lunchtime, we were given bread rations for three days. This brought another worry: where to hide it so it did not get stolen. The only place we had was in the suitcase, and that's where I put it.

On the third day in our new barrack I woke up at seven. I had had a long deep sleep. The potatoes made a big difference; it was wonderful to go to bed without feeling hungry. Mum was watching me and gave me a big smile and a good morning kiss.

It was about half-past seven when we were told that there would be no rollcall. That was good news, but also possibly bad news. When there was no rollcall, there was usually something more sinister in store for us. Mum decided to investigate.

'When the boys get back you should get some fresh air. I'm going now. I won't be long.'

She climbed down and soon, through the window, I saw her crossing the Appelplatz towards our old barrack. When Max and Jacky returned I headed outside. I had turned the corner of the barrack when I saw Mum coming towards me. She appeared nervous and shaky.

'What's the matter, Mum?' I asked when she was close enough.

'Something terrible is going to happen!' she said.

'What?'

For a moment Mum could not answer. I could see she was very upset.

'What is it?' I urged her.

'They say that the diamond group is going on a penalty transport today,' Mum said.

For a moment I was confused. Then the realisation dawned that our names had been added to that group.

'Oh, no! But perhaps they'll exclude us — and maybe there's no truth in the rumour.'

'No,' Mum said, 'it's true all right.'

I panicked. I took hold of Mum's arm. 'What are we going to do?'

Mum put her arms around me. 'Hush. Stay calm, then you can think more clearly. Somehow we'll manage. We aren't going, but Dad is. They're only sending the men away.'

By now, the whole camp was in commotion; the news had spread like wildfire. Max came outside and saw my distressed face, and Mum could no longer hold back her tears. He ran to her and buried his face in her chest with his arms tightly around her.

'What are we going to do?' he cried.

Mum stroked his hair while trying to compose herself.

'Look, there's Dad,' I said.

As if in a dream, I watched the small group of men downing their hats, faces turned right, in salute to the SS guard as they entered the camp. Dad spotted us at once and hurried toward us. No words were needed as Dad's eyes met Mum's. The misery they mirrored was unbearable. Dad's arms went around Mum. They stood very still, embracing each other without a word, the pain of the impending separation written on their faces.

When at long last Dad released her, he kissed Max and me and said to Max, 'Come with me to our barrack to pick up our suitcase and bedding. From now on you'll sleep with Mum. Let's go! They've given us an hour.'

Max and Dad left, and Mum and I went to the barrack to wait for them to return. Mum told Jacky the bad news while I opened the suitcase to pull out three rations of bread to give Dad. So this is why they gave us a three-day bread ration, I thought. How cunning they are. They had it all arranged, the filthy swines.

It didn't take long for Dad to return with Max. Dad carried his suitcase and Max carried a blanket and a sheet. Dad took the three rations of bread. Mum wanted to give him a jar of sugar, but Dad steadfastly refused.

'It's for my children. I won't take it,' he said.

No matter how Mum pleaded, he would not change his mind. One by one he embraced us and told us to be good and to look after Mum. We all scrambled down to the floor to escort Dad to the gate. As we were leaving the barrack, lots of women and men came up to Dad and wished him well.

Outside, I noticed how grey the sky was. Everything

looked grey. About two hundred men with their families had gathered near the gate and we joined them. A hush settled over the Appelplatz. Most people had done their crying in private. At the moment of departure it appeared that an inner strength had come to the surface. Although everyone was anguished with the knowledge that they might never see their loved ones again, with only a few exceptions they made an effort to look cheerful in order to give each other the courage to face the uncertain future.

We were standing close together when the SS guard called the names of the men to come forward.

Dad turned to Mum and said, 'Darling, take good care of yourself and the children, but most of all, stay alive. I will see you again soon. I am sure that the war will soon be over. I will find you.'

Mum could not speak; her eyes were burning with tears. Jacky and Max were crying. Dad kissed Mum and held her close, then he kissed the boys and told them to be good for Mum. At last he turned to me, and his warm brown eyes looked into mine.

'Hetty,' he said, 'you are the oldest. Look after your mother for me, and the boys.'

I nodded. I could not speak and he kissed me goodbye. Then his name was called. There was nothing we could do. He had to leave. A final kiss for Mum and he walked away from us towards the gate where his name was ticked off against the list by the SS officer. We saw him go through the gate to join the other men already standing there. Uncle Max was among them. Dad had been one of the last to go.

Every wife and child tried to get a last glimpse of their dear one and we vied for a position along the fence. The order was shouted and the men started to move.

'Goodbye! Goodbye!'

We called and waved to all the men who were forced to leave us, until they disappeared into the distance. Once the men had left, their wives and children cried bitterly. They did not have to pretend any longer.

Slowly the Appelplatz emptied. Silently, we walked towards our barrack. In my imagination I followed Dad on the road to the station where they would board the train, but to where? An immeasurable distance without horizon appeared in my mind. I could not see anything. It was void. Dad, where are you? My heart was calling out to him, but no answer came back. After climbing onto our bed, I dared to look at Mum for the first time. In her eyes I could see the pain. What could I say?

'Mum,' I said, 'Dad will be all right.'

'You think so?' Mum answered. Like a frightened child, she was asking for reassurance.

'I'm sure of it,' I told her. 'You mustn't let it get you down. We'll see him again soon. He said so and I know it. He's a survivor.' From somewhere the words came to me, and I was glad that Mum took comfort from them. Strangely, my own words also comforted me.

Mum lifted her head and saw the two boys who had sat silently while I talked to her. She embraced them both as one and said, 'We have to do it together now Dad is gone.'

The boys nodded their heads. Somehow, we would manage.

Later that day, we shared the last potatoes and ate some of our bread ration. We all felt desolate and depressed. We were all glad when it was time to go to sleep. We each found new positions as Max was sharing the bed now. Max slept at once. Mum lay awake for some time, then I could hear her steady breathing and knew she was asleep. I lay awake for many hours thinking of Dad and I prayed to God to look after my father.

After Mum left for work in the morning, Max lay next to me. We slept until half-past six and woke up when Jacky told us the coffee had arrived. We drank the brown water to get warm.

'Where do you think Dad is now?' Jacky asked.

I don't know,' I answered.

Silence fell between us. I took out a bread ration from the suitcase; it was brown and dry. I cut off three very thin slices, about a quarter of our daily ration. This had to last us until the soup arrived. Just as we prepared to go to rollcall we were told there would be no rollcall this morning, so the three of us remained sitting on top of our bed.

It was 5 December 1944, St Nicholas' Day, the day

that all children in Holland are spoiled with sweets and presents. I doubted we would be spoilt this year.

At about nine o'clock Mum walked into the barrack.

'What's the matter, Mum? Why have you come back from work?' I asked.

'We're going on a transport!' she said.

'What?' I was shocked, and a feeling of impending catastrophe took hold of me.

'We must pack our things now. We have to be ready at eleven,' Mum said.

Mum's quiet words subdued the panic. How strong she is, I thought. She knows she must stay calm for our sakes.

'God will look after us, believe me,' Mum said.

I was not so sure. How could God allow people to know such suffering as we had experienced?

I helped Mum to fold the blankets and sheets, and we packed them with the meagre remains of our clothing. Mum carefully placed our jars of sugar and the salt in between the folds of the blankets. We still had another hour to wait before going to the gate. We sat on our bed. We did not say much. We were torn between hope and despair. Perhaps we were going to a better camp. I did not want to think about the possibility that we could be sent to a worse place.

'We'd better go outside, then we can see what's happening,' Mum said.

Mum and I climbed down, and the boys handed the

suitcases to us. The woman from the lower bed climbed up to claim possession of our bed before anyone else could. Mum and I carried the suitcases as we walked towards the exit. Max and Jacky followed. We didn't go to the gate immediately, but stayed near the barrack. We could observe from this position what was taking place on the Appelplatz and at the gates. Lots of women with their luggage and their children had already assembled on the Appelplatz.

At ten minutes to eleven, Albela came to the gate and we could see Mr Weiss as well. Three SS officers arrived five minutes later. We noticed that some of the women had moved towards the gate. Suddenly we heard a commotion erupt.

A woman started to scream hysterically, 'My baby, my baby, I want my baby!'

Another woman cried, 'No! 'No!'

We could hear the SS yelling, 'Move on! Move on!'

'My God, we have to leave the children behind. They're not allowing them to come with us,' Mum said.

I was numb with horror.

'Quick Hetty, get back into the barrack with the suitcase, we have no time to lose!' Mum commanded.

The barrack was deserted; everybody was watching at the gate. In a few quick movements, Mum separated a blanket and her clothing into one of the suitcases. She also took one jar which was half full of sugar and put it in her case.

'Now Hetty, I want you and the boys to eat a spoonful of sugar now and then, but be very careful with it, because you can exchange it for bread or something you need. Promise me you will do this,' she said.

'Yes, Mum,' I said. I could feel the tremendous responsibility which now rested on my shoulders.

'Hetty, look after the boys for me,' Mum said again.

'Yes, Mum,' I promised. We both knew that our last minutes of being together were quickly ticking away.

'Oh,' Mum said, 'I nearly forgot. Here's the nit comb.' She pulled it out of the pocket of her coat. 'Keep your hair clean, and the boys' too.'

I nodded and put the comb in my pocket. During all these months in the camp, Mum had kept our hair free of lice. Mum took me in her arms and kissed me again and again. I clung to her. I knew she had to go soon. No tears had come to either of us. Our eyes were dry but our hearts were bleeding.

'Come,' Mum said, 'I must say goodbye to the boys.'

We picked up our suitcases and went outside to the boys. Mum embraced them. They were crying bitterly.

'Hush my darlings, you both must be big men now and listen to Hetty. She will look after you. You must stay together and go back to Amsterdam, to the Pomstra family, after the war is over.' Mum kissed them again and again.

'Are you going to take Mum to the gate?' she asked, as she slowly straightened up.

She picked up her suitcase and with the boys clinging to her coat, we slowly walked to the gate. When we were about five metres away, Mr Weiss gently separated the boys from Mum. She turned to give us a last kiss. The boys were now clinging to me, crying out their sorrow. I couldn't hold back my own tears any more as I watched Mum climb onto the back of the truck with her suitcase. It was like a nightmare seeing Mum leave in the same manner as Dad had just the day before.

When the truck started to move, Mum called out: 'Be good, my children, goodbye!'

We waved and called our goodbyes. Everybody was crying and our hearts were breaking.

Chapter 7

When the truck had disappeared into the distance, I turned around and noticed, for the first time, that about forty children were grouped near the fence. Most of them were under ten years of age. A few women from the hospital were caring for the two babies and the very small children.

'Are we going back to the barrack now?' I asked, turning to Mr Weiss, who had followed us to the fence.

'No, Hetty,' Mr Weiss said, 'a truck is coming for all the children in a moment. You're all going away.'

Hope flickered in my heart that we would follow Mum, but that was not to be.

Our tears had dried, but all the children, including myself, were in a state of shock. The cruelty of it all had left its mark. Little children were walking aimlessly around, crying out for their mothers. From somewhere a few bottles of milk arrived for the babies.

At last, at about four o'clock the truck arrived to take us away. Mr Weiss and some other men were allowed to help us onto the trucks. They lifted up the children one by one, but the babies were handed over to me and Eva; we were the oldest of the children.

With sad eyes, Mr Weiss waved us goodbye as the truck started to move. The children had stopped crying. The ride in the truck took their attention away from their misery. Our camp lay behind us and we passed the Häftling camp. Those poor creatures were still standing at rollcall. They must have been there for eight hours by now.

We went through the gate and into the camp reserved for the SS. The trucks slowed down and stopped in front of a building with big double doors. We were told to get out.

We were herded into the building, which turned out to be the SS garage. When we entered, we saw the luggage our mothers had taken with them. They must have been ordered to leave it behind in the garage. Soon the children had identified their mother's luggage and taken possession of it. After finding out the name of the baby I was holding, I asked the children to find his mother's suitcase, as we desperately needed to change his nappy. We made a little corner with a blanket so we could put the baby down. It was amazing how quickly the children found the suitcase. Eva offered to change the baby so I could attend to the other one. The children quickly brought me the suitcase that belonged to the second baby. Two girls of about ten offered to change her. The little ones of walking age all had wet pants and were crying their eyes out.

Again, I enlisted the children to find suitcases. It took some time to sort out and change them all. When I went through the suitcases left behind by the mothers, I felt like an intruder into the private belongings of other people, but I told myself the mothers would be happy that their children were being taken care of. I made sure that all belongings were returned to the right suitcases.

We had been in the garage for at least two hours. Nobody guarded us. We were all very tired. We had been on our feet since early in the morning without any food or drink. It was very cold outside and the light was fading fast. Stars appeared and the moon began to rise. As darkness settled in the garage, most of the children were terrified in the unfamiliar surroundings, especially as their mothers were not there to comfort them. They were cold and hungry. Pandemonium broke out. A chorus of voices screamed and screamed. Someone suggested that we all should cry out in unison, and as we were so desperate we tried to do it. On the count of three we all screamed in the hope that someone would hear us. We kept it up until our voices began to fail us.

By now it was very dark in the garage. The only light was from the moon through the open door. Nobody came near us. We huddled together and felt lost and forlorn. Through the darkness I felt my way to the door and looked out. There was no one in sight, the road was deserted. Some lights were burning in the SS quarters. The children kept screaming, it was ear-splitting. This was not just crying, it was the sound of desperation. We had lost our fathers and our mothers in a matter of two days and now, after having been left alone for hours in the garage, we believed we had been forgotten by the world.

Then suddenly a torch was shone into the garage. Two shadowy figures walked in and switched on the lights. What a sorry sight we must have been. About forty children huddled together in the corner with tear-stained faces. As I was the nearest one, the guards asked me where we came from. I told him that we had come from Sternlager at about four o'clock that afternoon. They conversed with each other, then one left. The man who stayed with us in the garage did not wear the uniform of the SS; his uniform was green. He looked about fifty years old and held his rifle in readiness. When the light had been switched on, the crying had stopped for a little while, and during the lull we heard a St Nicholas party in progress in the SS barracks. The SS were singing St Nicholas songs at the top of their voices.

The crying started again; when one child stopped another would start. They were bewildered and without hope. I approached the guard and politely asked him what the time was. He told me it was a quarter past nine. He asked me if I could stop the children from crying. My German was very limited, so it took me some time to understand what he was saying. I told him in broken German and sign language that they were very hungry and tired.

The guard looked ill at ease amid this misery. After he understood what I had tried to tell him he nodded his head and said, 'Don't go away. I will come back.' He then left the garage. I didn't understand what he meant by 'Don't go away.' Where would I go?

I walked back to where the small children were huddled together on the floor. They were totally exhausted by their ordeal. The worst of the wailing had quietened down. They were spent. Some of the little ones were even asleep on the cold concrete floor. They were worn out and, mercifully, sleep had taken over. I told the older boys to cover the little ones with blankets as the night was really cold. I told the other children not to cry but to try and sleep.

Everybody was so very tired from the long, long hours on our feet, the traumatic upheaval we had experienced, as well as having had nothing to eat all day. It became quiet now. Most of the little ones were sleeping. The older ones were talking to each other in low tones, all afraid to go to sleep. I was tired but not sleepy.

About an hour after the guard had left us, he returned with two male prisoners who each carried a large carton. At the same time, a car arrived. Two men entered the garage with their arms full of blankets. I recognised the men from our camp. They told us when Mr Weiss had found out that we were being held in the SS garage, he arranged for the blankets to be delivered to us. We were very glad as now the older children could have some covers as well.

When the men left, the guard called me over and pointed to the two cartons standing on the floor. He nodded his head in approval, motioning me to look into the boxes. I hesitated. I did not trust him. I walked slowly towards the cartons, and then looked at the guard again. He didn't say a word but made a movement with his head, indicating for me to look inside them. I opened the first box, removed a paper cover and could not believe my eyes. Under the paper were thick slices of white bread sandwiches filled with butter and sugar. I lifted my eyes to look at the guard, too afraid to touch anything. He nodded approval, then turned away, making out he saw nothing.

I called out to Max and some of the older boys and girls who were still awake. They came towards me and, whispering, I told them of the heavenly gift the guard had brought us. We each took a sandwich from the box. I told some of the boys to take a sandwich to all the other children who were still awake but were bedded down for the night. We were so hungry, what a party we had! Fresh white bread with butter and sugar. For ten months we had eaten only dry brown bread a quarter of the size of one of these thick slices — our rations for twenty-four hours.

I looked into the second box, which was also filled to

the top with those beautiful sandwiches. I contemplated waking the sleeping children to let them have their share, but decided against it. Sleep meant forgetfulness and the sandwiches would keep until they woke up.

Max, Bram and Iesy came back for a second sandwich. I let them have one but told them that although there were plenty more, we had better keep something for the next day. Looking at the faces of the children while they were eating, I told myself that from this moment on I would believe in St Nicholas. He did indeed make children happy on his birthday.

It was now half-past eleven. The chilly outside air penetrated the garage. Trucks could be heard coming down the road. They stopped in front of the garage, then two SS officers and a female guard entered. Most of the children who had been asleep woke up. We were told to move onto the trucks. The children, so rudely awakened, started to cry again.

I went on the first truck with a lot of little children and Max and Jacky. I carried our suitcase, and Max carried the suitcase that Mum had left behind. The last to board our truck was Bram, his sister Bella, and Iesy. Bram and Iesy each carried a box of sandwiches. The female guard came with us on the truck.

The truck drove fast. We had no idea where we were going. The night was jet black, the moon had disappeared behind the clouds. It was midnight. Nobody spoke, even the crying had stopped. I noticed that we left the camp through the main gate and that we were on the road towards Celle, but then the truck turned left and we seemed to drive aimlessly around in circles through the heather. For hours we drove like this. The moon had come from behind the clouds and through the open rear of the truck I could see the vast expanse of the Lüneburg Heath. There was no one in sight and no sound to be heard, only the engines of the trucks breaking the deathly silence. Then the trucks stopped. The female guard left the back of our truck and the driver from the second truck came over to our driver. We could hear them discussing something. Our driver seemed very upset as we could hear him say, '*Nein, nein*,' a few times but we could not follow the conversation. What were they talking about? Were they going to kill us? We were silent, feeling the danger around us.

After about ten minutes of arguing, the female guard climbed back in our truck and we started to drive again. I realised that we were driving back in the direction of the camp. We re-entered Belsen and passed the Sternlager. Near the end of the road we turned left and stopped. We were pulled out of the truck by the female guard before two tall, strong women prisoners arrived to take over from her. They wore prison clothes with scarves around their bald heads. On seeing those scary, skinny women, the children started to cry again.

The second truck arrived and its lights lit up the area.

When our truck started to move away, one of the women prisoners went up to the driver and asked what they should do with the children.

'I don't care,' he said. 'They can burn in hell.'

The trucks drove away and we were left in the darkness. The children were terrified and began wailing again. After my eyes became accustomed to the darkness I could see the vague outline of a barrack in front of us. A woman prisoner told us to enter the building, which looked ominous in the dark. Slowly we moved forward. I felt very scared, but did not dare show it.

When we entered the building my heart skipped a beat. There was what appeared to be a very long corridor. It was pitch-dark, and at the end stood an old woman holding up a kerosene lamp. If ever there was an image of a wicked witch, then this woman was certainly it. The sight of her scared the children again and they buried their faces in my coat. The figure at the end of the corridor did not move. She was standing deathly still holding up the lamp, which cast her shadow behind her. I realised we had to move forward. The children were hanging onto me like a dead weight. I raised my voice and told them very firmly to come with me, and that they did not have to be afraid. They had the choice of coming with me or I would leave them alone. This had the desired effect, they loosened their grip to allow me to move forward. I freed my hand from the child who had been holding it tightly and shoved the little ones behind me to protect them as much as possible with my body. Slowly we moved towards the figure. As we came closer I realised she was standing beside a doorway. A faint light spilled out from the opening. Now we had come very close to her, she pointed to the doorway without saying a word. Trying to keep as much distance between us and the witch, we stepped through it.

What a relief! The room was clean and had about ten double bunks where we could sleep. The beds took up half the room and the other half was empty space. Two chairs were standing against the wall. A bare bulb hanging from the ceiling spread sparse light, but enough for us to see everything. The children were also relieved and let go of my coat. Some had already moved towards the beds. I dropped my suitcase on the floor when I heard more screaming in the corridor and knew the children from the second truck had just seen the witch.

I quickly returned to the corridor so the terrified children could see me. I told them to come in, everything was okay. Soon all the children were assembled in the room. Eva and another girl put the babies on a bed. In the meantime, female prisoners carried in our suitcases and other belongings and stacked them in the middle of the open area of the room. Then they left and we were alone.

Eva and I took control. We told everybody to find a bed and go to sleep. Those who were too small to climb up were assisted by the bigger boys. Amazingly, both babies were asleep although they'd had nothing to eat. We had given them some water earlier, and that must have filled their tummies up.

Then one little boy said, 'I have to go to the toilet.'

We looked at each other. In our misery, we had overlooked that fact. What to do? Going outside into the long dark corridor was out of the question. We did not have any idea where we were or where to find the latrines.

My gaze fell on a large green cooking pan in the luggage. I told one of the boys to get the pan, which had a lid. I got everyone out of bed again to use the pan. In the process, we found that some of the children had wet their pants already. It had been such a long day. Eva and I slipped those children out of their wet clothing and put them back to bed with bare bottoms, covering them with the blankets. Thank God no one had wet their bed yet.

We were all on the point of collapse, so I suggested we go to sleep. All the bunks except the one nearest to the door were occupied. In some beds, four children were sleeping, two on each end. The bigger children had sorted their beds out and chosen their own partners. I had chosen the double top bed which I shared with Max, Jacky and Louky. I left the light on, so if someone woke up to use the pan, they could see where they were going. I also felt safer that way. I must have fallen asleep as soon as I lay down. It was three o'clock in the morning.

I was awoken by Emile, who called me to tell me the pan was full. Light was filtering through the window. It was a wintry grey morning. Most of the children were still asleep from sheer exhaustion. Emile told me that he had opened the unlocked door on the far end of the room.

'It takes you outside,' he said.

I woke Max and Louky and told them to take the cooking pan outside and empty it.

'Try not to wake the children,' I said.

Max and Louky were still sleep-weary when they climbed down to do what I had asked them. It was amazing how all the children accepted my authority. I suppose I represented the mother they had just lost. They had unreservedly put their trust in me and without hesitation I had taken it upon myself to look after them as best as I could.

Emile opened the door for Max and Louky and the three of them disappeared out of sight. They soon returned with the empty pan, just in time, as the children woke up and there was a big demand for it.

The babies woke up and started to cry. They were very hungry. By now, we had found some small pots and containers in the suitcases, and I sent Emile outside to find a tap to fill containers with water. We also found some small bowls. I put some of the white bread with sugar and butter in two bowls and, with the water Emile brought me, I managed to soften the bread into some sort of porridge for the babies. Eva and another girl had found some clean clothing for them and had changed them by the time I had the porridge ready. There were plenty of helpers ready to feed the babies.

For breakfast, with the help of Iesy, we gave each child half a sandwich. The other half, we told them, they could have at night. Cold water was the only drink we had. Silence fell as everyone enjoyed their sandwich. Then we left the children to do their own thing.

Emile went outside with another boy to do some exploring and to find a toilet block. They soon came back, as it was very cold outside. They had found a latrine not far from our barrack. The biggest children could manage this, but not the little ones, so we decided they should use the cooking pan during the day as well.

Iesy, Eva, Louky, Bram, Max and I met to discuss our position. We sat on top of my bed. The double bunk allowed us to sit in a circle. There were forty-four children and we were the oldest, so we had to take care of the little ones. Iesy suggested that we go through all the luggage to see if there was any food in it, and if we found anything, to put it all together. We agreed. The boys climbed down to go through the luggage.

The children did not cry any more as they felt secure within our group. We had a roof over our heads, we had beds and there was enough food for today. Some younger boys started to help with the search through the suitcases.

When they found something, they brought it to me on the bed. When the last suitcase was searched, we took stock: two packets of biscuits as hard as rocks, half a packet of sweet biscuits, half a tin of tea, half a tin of chocolate powder, a small bag of soap powder and a near-empty tin of milk powder.

The boys came up onto the bed to survey the goods. It would not still our hunger in the days to come. I put it all in our suitcase and took it into my control. I told the boys to stack the luggage against the wall in a far corner of the room. They were glad to have something to do and made a good job of it. This way, we had some more space.

The day dragged by. No one came near us. It was as if we were in a world of our own. At least we had a chance to recover from the trauma of the day before. When daylight started to fade, with the help of Iesy and Eva I handed out the other half of the sandwiches. For the babies I made porridge again. We still had about three-quarters of a box of sandwiches left for the next day. For security reasons, it was placed on top of my bed. Everybody went to bed early and it wasn't long before we were all asleep.

After breakfast the next day some of the boys went outside to explore. It was very quiet in this part of the camp. When they came back they said there were a few more barracks nearby, but most were empty and no one was around.

I hadn't ventured outside yet, as the little children

needed me. They looked so forlorn and although the crying in unison had stopped, now and then a little one would cry for his or her mummy. The ten-month-old baby, Phillipje, was very quiet. He would just lie there and stare into space. Now and then a smile touched his little mouth when I spoke gently to him, or tickled him under his chin. He emanated sadness and must have missed his mother terribly. I hadn't seen him sit up yet. He wasn't skinny, so his mother must have been able to feed him somehow. The other baby, a girl, was about twelve months old. And then there was little Robby, who was about three years old. He had such a pretty face, blond hair and blue eyes. He did not say one word, even when he was spoken to. He looked so lost and lonely, poor little Robby. I sometimes gave him a cuddle, but never a smile came to his eyes. It was as if he had built a wall around himself. I decided I would keep a special eye on him and one day I might gain his confidence. Slowly I got to know the names of most of the children.

You cannot keep young girls and boys indoors forever, and groups of three or four would go outside and return a while later. They reported that the latrine was brand new, so it appeared we were the first inhabitants in this part of the camp.

Later in the afternoon I had to go out myself. It was so peaceful here, not a sound could be heard. The sky was light grey, the air crisp but not cold. I was glad to be out in the open air and filled my lungs with it. When I returned to the barrack I asked if anyone had come to see us. The answer was negative. I could not understand why no one had come to see us or brought us food. Someone wanted to forget about us, I thought, but I kept this thought to myself. No use worrying the others with it.

It was about four o'clock when all the children returned from outside. They had discovered that the building where the shoe detail worked was situated between our old camp and the one we were in now. This at least established our position. They also reported that they had found the gate to the main road, which was open, with no one there to guard it. They hadn't ventured outside the gate although no one was in sight there either.

Night was falling. Iesy brought down the box of sandwiches. Everybody lined up in a queue, which slowly passed Iesy and me as we handed each child the last half of the white bread sandwiches left in the box. When we finished, there were four halves left. Iesy and I decided to keep these to feed the babies the next day. For a while we were sitting around talking to each other. A few little girls were sitting close to me and I gave them a hug. Eva was reading a story from a book she had found in the luggage to a group of children who were listening intently. How idyllic it looks, I thought. One would think we were on holidays.

It was pitch-dark outside, not a star could be found in the sky.

‘I think it’s time to go to sleep,’ I told everybody. ‘It’s getting cold, so get under your blankets.’

No one undressed. We slept in our clothing except for the babies, who had been changed after their meal. We had to find a way to wash the babies’ things, as soon we would have nothing to change them into. One empty suitcase was used to store the soiled baby goods. But that problem I will somehow resolve tomorrow, I thought, as I also climbed up on my bed.

Soon the children were asleep except for Iesy and me. We sat on the end of my bed talking in whispers. Iesy was intelligent and in him I found support. He was about thirteen years old, a year younger than myself. I told Iesy of my concern that no one had come to see us and that no food whatsoever was brought to us. We felt trapped. Could we go through the gates to get help? We really didn’t know what to do.

‘If no one comes tomorrow, I’ll call out to the guard in the tower and tell him we are alone here,’ I said to Iesy.

Iesy thought that much too dangerous and advised me against it.

‘I understand that,’ I said, ‘but what are we going to do? All the sandwiches are finished and we have nothing to eat tomorrow!’

We talked and talked about ways to get out of our predicament, but couldn’t see a solution.

Chapter 8

Iesy was just moving away to his bed when the door opened and two women entered. They were the first people to come and see us in two days. The shorter of the two was a strong woman: her blue blouse strained over her chest and her short sleeves revealed strong arms. Neither of them showed signs of hunger or starvation. They were not dressed like prisoners. They both wore black skirts and leather boots. For a moment, the two women observed the surroundings and then the short one spoke to me in Polish. When she saw that I could not understand it, she asked in German, 'Jewish children?'

For a moment I hesitated before nodding. She spoke urgently to the other woman, then said, 'Hunger,' and made a movement with her hand towards her mouth to make sure I understood. I thought it advisable not to tell her that we'd had sandwiches tonight, so I nodded.

'I'll come back,' she said, and then they left. It had all happened so quickly.

Iesy climbed back onto my bed.

'What was that?' he asked.

I told him what had happened.

'What do you think of it?' he asked.

'I don't know. I don't like the fact that she asked me if the children were Jewish.'

Iesy nodded.

'I hope we don't have to move tonight, the children are sleeping so nicely,' I said.

'We'd better go to sleep. Sitting up isn't helping us. Tomorrow, we'll see what happens,' Iesy said.

He went back to his bed carefully, so he would not wake up his bedmate. As I lay down next to Max, under the blanket, I was thinking about the two women. I was amazed they did not feel the cold. They both wore cotton blouses with short sleeves, and yet they looked strong and healthy. They still had their hair and each wore a head scarf in the manner of a Russian peasant. I had no doubt that the shorter woman was the boss.

I woke to hear footsteps coming down the corridor. Immediately I sat upright, my whole body tense, afraid of what might happen next. I could hear voices. The footsteps came nearer and then the door opened. The two women had returned and behind them, four women prisoners carried two twenty-litre food containers. The short woman told the prisoners to place the food containers in the middle of the room, then ordered them to leave. From the top of my bed, I watched with great relief. When I'd heard them coming down the corridor, I was worried that we might have to move again.

At the door, the shorter woman looked up at me and said, 'Start eating.'

The noise created by the arrival of the food had woken up a few children. Iesy, Max, Bram and Emile had left their beds already to investigate the food containers. I climbed down to have a look. Iesy tried to open the lid of one of the containers but without success. The catch stayed firmly shut. By now, Bram had joined us. He took hold of the levers but only managed to lift the lid a little bit, not high enough to release the spring, so the lid would stay open. Bram let go.

'All right,' I said, 'when Bram tries to lift the handle again, you, Iesy and Max, put your hands on the levers to stop them from springing back. I will count to three and together you will pull it up.'

Max and Iesy placed themselves in position. Bram put his hand on the lever and said, 'Are you ready?'

'Yes!' Max and Iesy said.

Bram started to pull with all his might. When the levers came up enough to allow Max and Iesy to place a hand around them, I started to count, 'One … two … three.' The boys started to force the lever up with all the strength they possessed. Their faces were contorted with the pressure. They were not very strong. Ten months of slow starvation had taken its toll. Slowly the lever came up until, with a mighty click, it released its hold on the containers. Out of breath but excited by their victory, it took them only a second to lift the second lever, as the pressure had been released when the first lever was opened.

By now, more children had awoken and come out of their beds to find out what was happening. Iesy lifted the lid. A beautiful aroma penetrated our nostrils. Inside the container was a thick creamy potato soup. We could not believe our good luck. In no time everybody who was up and about produced a soup bowl and helped themselves to a generous portion of soup. We sat on the floor, close to the containers, as if afraid that they would disappear. It tasted so good! No one spoke as we relished this delicious food, food we could only have dreamed about during the past ten months. Through the steam rising from his soup bowl Iesy's eyes met mine; we knew we did not have to worry about how to feed the children for the next two days.

Bram placed the lid on the container but did not close the clips, to make it easier to get it open in the morning. Iesy put a small suitcase on the lid to keep it down firmly so the soup would stay warm. After that, everybody went to bed and within seconds we were all asleep.

The next morning I woke up to find the suitcase on my bed open. I was sure I had closed the lid the night before. I went through the contents: half the sweet biscuits were missing. I called Iesy and Max over to discuss the matter. I was very angry. Most of us were not hungry the night before, so who could it be? If we were to survive, we could not tolerate pilfering. Louky, who had climbed up on the bed, interrupted our conversation.

'Hetty, a little boy said that Emile did it.'

I remembered that Emile had done something like this before. I had to be sure, so I told Louky to bring this little boy to me. Louky climbed down and returned with the boy.

From the top of my bed I asked the little boy, whose name I did not know, 'Tell me, how do you know that Emile stole the biscuits?'

'I saw him eat the biscuits early this morning,' the little boy answered.

'Are you sure?' I asked him again.

'Yes, I'm sure,' he replied.

'It's true,' a little girl agreed.

'If you make these accusations, you have to be very sure of it,' I said, turning to the girl.

'Well,' the little girl said, 'it is true. I saw it too! He ate three biscuits and he was sitting in that corner.' She pointed to the end of the last row of the beds and I realised that the place she was pointing to was out of view from my position.

'What are we going to do with Emile?' I asked Iesy and Max.

'Wait until we hear what he has to say,' Iesy said.

'You're right,' I said. 'We'll listen to what he has to say.'

The other children in the room were well aware of what was happening. They were wise at an early age, these children, and most of them had learned to deal with the hard times and crises which had taken place from day to day since they had arrived in Belsen. The happy mood which had prevailed because they were going to get a good breakfast of potato soup, had now turned into a depressing atmosphere. In all this unpleasant mess, I had forgotten to feed the kids.

I came down from the bed and told everybody to line up to receive their soup. Iesy moved the suitcase from the top of the container and opened the lid. The soup was still warm. The children were holding up their bowls and Eva was filling them up one by one. Soon everybody had been served. Iesy and I were the last.

I was just sitting down on a suitcase to eat my soup when Louky and Jacky returned with Emile. Not wanting to spoil the happy mood, I told the three boys to get their bowls and help themselves.

When everyone was finished I quickly got Iesy, Max, Louky, Bram and Eva together and we all climbed onto my bed. We sat in a circle and looked very serious, as the responsibility of dealing with this matter now rested on our shoulders. I called Emile to come up. Emile sat opposite us. While he was settling down, I studied his face. Emile was quite a good-looking boy. He had nice black hair and made a very decent impression, but there was something about him which made him appear distant and impenetrable. I told Emile that biscuits were missing from the suitcase and that it was alleged that he had stolen them during the night.

To my surprise, Emile immediately admitted he had done it. He showed no remorse, only a deadpan look. I asked him why he did it, but he just shrugged his shoulders.

'You know what you've done is very serious?' Iesy asked.

Emile did not answer, but looked straight ahead. We did not know what to say.

'You'd better get down, Emile! But don't go away!' I told him.

Emile climbed down and the five of us turned to each other and started to discuss the situation in low voices. What could we do? We couldn't let him get away with it as this would not be a good example for the other children. I believed that whatever punishment we meted out, we would never cure Emile of his affliction.

Different methods were proposed and rejected until Iesy said, 'What if we let Emile empty the pan every morning for a week? It's an unpleasant task and it may teach him a lesson.'

We all agreed this was the best idea. Louky called Emile to come up again and he was informed of our decision. I asked Emile if he agreed and he said, 'Yes.'

It was about eleven o'clock in the morning when the door opened and the two women who had visited us before and brought the potato soup, entered our room accompanied by two other women. We immediately noticed an air of authority. Later we found out that one of the women was second in charge to the camp elder of all the prisoners. She was a mature prisoner who had been in Auschwitz for many years. The other woman was a doctor.

The children, who had until this moment been happily chatting away, fell silent. As young as they were, they recognised danger in a flash. I was washing little Johnny's face when they came in, and I pulled him close to me for protection, but the women did not take much notice of us. After about five minutes discussion, they started to leave.

As they were passing through the door, the woman who had brought the soup for us before turned to me and said, 'Do you need more soup?'

Without hesitation I said, 'Yes.'

'I will bring it later,' she said.

After they left, it took us a few minutes to be ourselves again, and we were glad they had gone.

'What do you think about that?' Iesy asked me.

'I don't know,' I answered. 'I only hope we don't have to move again.'

The back door was open and we could see a column of women prisoners walking past towards the empty barracks.

'It looks like the empty barracks will be occupied,' Iesy said. 'I'll go out and see what's happening.'

'You do that,' I said. 'I'll stay with the children. If you see any of them outside, tell them to come back. Anything can happen outside and we'd better stay in.'

It was still early in the evening, but there was nothing to do other than hang around on the cold floor so everyone went to bed early.

How safe we feel in this room, I thought, as I crawled under the blanket with my clothes on. Maybe she was our guardian angel, this woman whose name I did not know, who brought the food each day. I was scared of her but I must find out her name.

I woke up the next morning just as the dawn was lifting. Max sat up in a flash and said, 'Emile has to take the pan out.' The night before, we'd put it up on the empty bed.

With heavy, sleepy eyes, Emile got out of bed. From the top of the bed Max and Jacky carefully lowered the nearly full pan to Emile, who waited below with arms and hands stretched into the air to receive the pan. Expecting problems, I went down to direct operation 'pan lift'. I cautioned Max and Jacky to be careful as I didn't want a mess on the floor. Looking at Emile as he stood there, I did not think he could carry the weight of the pan on his own and I could foresee a disaster.

'Okay?' Max asked.

'Yes,' Emile said.

At this, Max released his grip but a fraction earlier than Jacky. The pan unbalanced slightly, spilling some of the contents over Emile and on the floor. Despite the mishap, Emile kept hold of the pan, preventing the rest of the contents from spilling out. He staggered back, still holding the pan.

'Put it down!' I yelled at Emile.

With a bang, Emile dropped the pan onto the floor, spilling more in the process.

'Louky, go with Emile to empty the pan,' I said.

Now the weight was divided between the two boys, the danger of spilling more had passed. Someone held open the back door to let Emile and Louky out, and we noticed that during the night it had snowed. The pristine white of the snow contrasted sharply with the grey clouds. It was dead still outside, not a sound could be heard.

As a result of the drama with the pan, all the children had woken up. They got excited when they saw the snow and wanted to go outside and play in it. I told them to have their breakfast first and then they could play while I cleaned up the resulting mess from the pan. It was a pleasure to see their clear eyes and rosy cheeks when they came in an hour later.

The day passed uneventfully and soon the evening meal was served. I sent up a silent prayer of thanks. We had been left alone. We had good food and good shelter.

Chapter 9

One day followed the next and we settled into a routine. Those who were allocated to do certain chores could now do them without supervision, and we had plenty to eat. The constant quest for food was removed. The children had accepted that they could not be with their mothers. Instead, they had adopted me as a substitute. Whenever a mishap occurred, they came to me for comfort. Whenever there was a problem, I had to sort things out. They trusted me implicitly and I did my best not to let them down.

We had not seen anybody for days. It looked as if the SS had forgotten our existence. Then, on the ninth day after our arrival, the two women returned to advise us that early the next morning, all children up to and including the age of thirteen were going to a new barrack, where they would be cared for by them. They told me that all luggage would be collected, and needed to be ready by eight o'clock the next day. This created an upheaval. The children became scared again. They had only just settled in and were beginning to feel secure. All day they came to me for reassurance, but when they found out that I could not come with them, as I was now fourteen, they really panicked. I tried to pacify them, and show them a happy face, but inside I was not so happy, especially as Max and Jacky had to go with them. I hid my anxiety from the children but discussed the position with Eva, whose little sister had to go as well. Iesy and Louky also had to go and I was desolate.

Eva and I decided to sort out the children's belongings and put them back into the right suitcases ready for their departure the next morning. This kept us busy until halfway through the afternoon. The suitcases were stacked neatly in the middle of the room ready to be taken away. Eva and I did not trust the two women and kept some clothing stored in cases which had been placed in a corner in the top of my double bed and covered with a blanket to hide them. This meant that Louky and Jacky had to sleep on another bed that night. We went to bed early, worn out by the emotion of the day.

Surprisingly, the children slept well, but I did not. For hours I stared out of the window across from my bed. The darkness of the night reflected my feelings. No stars were shining. A reflection of light might have given me some hope for the future. The uncertainty of our existence overwhelmed me as the hours dragged by. Max stirred next to me and opened his eyes.

'Can't you sleep?' he whispered.

'No,' I replied. 'Promise me, Max, that you'll look after Jacky.'

Max nodded. He took hold of my hand on top of the blanket. 'I promise,' he said, 'now try to get some sleep. You must be strong for tomorrow.'

I managed to smile at him, realising that he must be worried about me staying behind.

'I'll try,' I said. 'Now you go to sleep again.'

Max turned over onto his side and, within seconds, was sleeping peacefully. Sleep would not come for me and I was glad when first light arrived.

Carefully, trying not to wake Max, I slithered out of bed and walked to the back door. I went outside, closing the door gently behind me. I could see the sky lightening in the east, and the contours of the fence and watchtowers became visible. It was so quiet outside. Only the sounds of the guards and the dogs broke the silence as they patrolled the outside of the fence. I leaned with my back against the wall of the barrack and took deep breaths of the cold fresh air into my lungs. I lifted my head to the heavens and prayed that God would look after my two brothers and all the children who were going to leave in a few hours time. Tears were running down my face. I felt so helpless.

The door right next to me opened and Emile came out. He was startled to encounter me so early in the morning. His sudden appearance made me get a grip on myself.

'Where are you going?' I asked.

'To the washhouse.'

'Don't be long,' I told him, 'We're having an early breakfast.'

'Okay,' he said, as he walked past me.

I stood looking after him for a while. What a strange boy he is, I thought. What was he doing up so early in the morning? What was he up to now?

The door opened again. This time it was Louky.

'Oh, there you are,' he said. 'Everybody's looking for you. Some of the children want their breakfast already.'

I quickly wiped my eyes with the back of my hands to make sure no traces of tears showed on my face. When I came back inside, everybody was up. Eva had dressed the little ones, who were sitting neatly in a row on a blanket on the floor. I told Iesy and Bram to open the container of food which had arrived yesterday. What a surprise! It contained rice cooked in milk with lots of sugar in it. This put our departure out of our minds for the moment, we were so delighted. Soon everybody had been served and when someone wanted a second helping, I let them have it.

After the bowls had been washed, we used the sandwich box to pack them. The children were ready and an uneasy silence had fallen between us now that their departure was near. I moved slowly past the row of children on the floor and, kneeling down with each child, I told them to be good and to listen to the Sisters. I had adopted that name for the two women to make them sound more friendly. I told the children not to be afraid, as the 'Sisters' would give them food and they would not be hungry any more.

'Will you come to see us soon, Hetty?' one little girl asked.

'Of course!' I promised as I hugged her.

The last precious hour seemed to have gone by fast, as all of a sudden, the women arrived for the children. Because I had prepared the children for this moment, they remained calm and, as I had hoped, they showed no panic. I told them to form themselves into a line and to go with the women. Eva decided to go with them some of the way. Iesy came over to me and hugged me. He was always so demonstrative.

'Look after yourself, Hetty,' he said, and kissed me on both cheeks.

I nodded. My throat was closed. I could not answer immediately, but I somehow managed to say, 'Take care of the children, they trust you.'

'I will,' Iesy answered.

He let go of me. One by one, the children left the room. Only Max and Jacky remained. I embraced them both and kissed them goodbye. I walked them to the door. Jacky held tightly to my arm and while loosening his hold gently, I told him that he was grown up now and must look after himself.

'Keep yourself warm, darling, and stay close to Max. Stay close to each other.'

A final kiss for both of them, and I told them to hurry after the children.

'I will come to see you,' I called after them.

Max and Jacky turned once to wave goodbye from a distance and I waved back with a smile on my face, but when I went back inside, the tears came freely. I was at the end of my strength. I climbed on top of my bed and cried until I had no more tears left. I felt lost and alone. The room was empty except for some of the suitcases which still had to be collected. Eva had not returned yet. A thousand thoughts crowded my head. Where was my father? Where was my mother? And now my brothers were gone. I felt abandoned. The stillness of the room was ominous. I looked at all the empty beds and started to cry again.

The women returned for the last of the luggage. They looked terrible in their grey striped dresses. Their cheeks were hollow, their eyes deep in their sockets. They scared me. Their claw-like hands carried the cases. They were so thin. Where did they get the strength to work so hard, I wondered? Outside the door I could see a kapo who told them to hurry up and, like zombies, they responded. They also took the containers of food and the clean pan. I was glad I had stayed behind, otherwise they would have taken the cases on my bed as well. After they left I crawled under my blanket and tried to get some rest. I had no wish to go outside. Slowly I became warmer until, mercifully, I fell asleep.

When Eva returned she told me that the children had been taken to a barrack at the far end of our camp and the two women were looking after them.

'How far is it?' I asked.

'Not far. Tomorrow I'll go out and try to find us something to eat. There's no one at the gate. I'll walk to the kitchen and see what I can organise,' Eva said, yawning.

'Do you think that's wise?' I asked.

'Maybe not,' she answered, 'but I'll give it a try.'

Soon after, Eva went to bed. She plonked herself down, shoes and all. It had been a hard day for her.

'See you in the morning, goodnight.'

Eva turned on her side and was asleep within a minute. As there was nothing else to do, I crawled under my blanket again. Even if I could not sleep, at least I could keep warm. I pulled the blanket tightly around me. The room was colder than before, the natural body heat of so many children had made the temperature more bearable. I missed them and wondered how they were sleeping now.

The room was very still and again and again my eyes wandered over the empty beds, while I debated whether I should go to see the children tomorrow and whether I would be allowed to do this. I felt scared and insecure. During the past few days, it had become clear to me that although life in the previous camp was not so good, we did have some protection from Albela and the elders. This section of Belsen had different rules. It was run by very cruel kapos and only the strong and the devious would survive. I must try to get some sleep, I told myself.

'Hetty, wake up.'

I opened my eyes and saw Eva standing below my bed.

'I'm going now,' she said. 'I'll see you when I get back.'

'Okay, be careful.'

Bram also emerged from his bed. Until now I had not taken much notice of Bram, as I had been busy with the younger children. He was tall for his age, about sixteen or seventeen years old. His cheeks were hollow and he had high cheekbones and a pointy chin, which made his face look like a triangle. He avoided eye contact when I spoke to him. He was a bit strange and I felt that I had no connection with him.

'I wonder how Bella is,' Bram said, looking around the room.

I saw a sad look in his face. Perhaps I'm misjudging him, I thought. He does care for his sister. Soon Bram left, and I was alone. I decided to go for a walk. I had not ventured further than the toilet block before now. Before I left, I covered the suitcases with blankets. I knew I took a risk leaving the sugar jars unguarded, but I could not stay inside all the time.

The weather was gloomy. Grey, low-hanging clouds did not let the sunshine through. Our section of the camp looked deserted. When I passed the toilet block, I saw a woman using the outside tap. On my approach, she lifted her head. I had stopped with the intention of having a chat, but she went back to her chore and ignored me. I continued on. I followed the road in the direction Eva had shown me the night before, which led to the hospital.

There was not a sound, it was eerie. It was as if I was all alone in the world. I came to the building which I thought was the hospital. I stood for a while looking at it. Clean red bricks, high windows and no sign of life. Where was everybody? I started to feel very uncomfortable. Then a door opened and a tall SS officer came out of the building with a woman who was immaculately dressed in a dark blue suit. The two were in deep conversation and didn't notice me. I decided it was better to move on.

As I walked further along the road, two women appeared from behind the trees and walked towards me. They walked arm in arm as though they were on a Sunday stroll. As they drew near, one of the women pointed at me.

'That's Maurice's daughter,' she said.

Then I recognised them: Aunty Beth and Sonja's mother.

'How are you, darling?' Sonja's mother asked. 'What are you doing here?'

I told them how Mum and Dad had been sent away and Max and Jacky had gone to another barrack yesterday.

'Do you know which barrack the children are in?' I asked.

'Yes,' Sonja's mother said, 'it's there behind the trees. Have you got something to eat for us, Hetty?' she asked.

'No,' I answered.

'What about some salt?' Sonja's mother asked.

For a moment I hesitated as I looked at them. Aunty Beth was not in a good state. She was so skinny and had not said a word.

'Wait here,' I told Sonja's mother. 'I'll get you some salt.'

I walked quickly back to our room. With some effort, I extracted my suitcase from the others and opened it. I found the jar of salt, shook some out onto a piece of paper and then folded it carefully. This way, not a grain of salt would be lost. When I was finished, I closed the lid and left my suitcase where it was on the bed, as I did not have the strength to put it back between the other cases.

I handed the packet of salt over to Sonja's mother, who quickly hid it inside her dress. She thanked me very much and then walked away with Aunt Beth. It was the last time I saw Sonja's mother.

I continued my walk. Around the corner from the cluster of trees I saw three barracks. I stood still. Which of the barracks would be the children's? Nothing I could see gave me any indication that the children were there. I approached slowly. The first barrack was deserted so I advanced to the second one and peeped through the window. This was it. I saw most of the children sitting around a long table. Some were sitting in the middle of the room on the floor. A few little ones were crying their eyes out. The short woman went over to a crying child, but when she was bending down the child started to cry even more loudly.

On straightening up, the woman saw me peering through the window. She asked through the glass what I was doing there.

I told her, 'Brother, brother.' She opened the door for me and asked me to come in.

Once inside, I surveyed the room. The bunks for the children were placed in two rows, along the length of the right wall. A corner on the left near the door was divided off with two bunks and to my dismay some of our blankets had been used to shut off the corner for privacy. As soon as I entered, a horde of children encircled me and grabbed hold of me. They were so happy to see me! The children who had been crying stopped and nearly pushed each other over in order to touch me. They were hanging onto my arms and all talking at once. I told everyone to sit around the tables and I would tell them a story. For two hours I kept them busy and made them feel good.

I decided not to overstay my welcome and made a move

to go, but not before I had a talk with Max and Jacky. I asked them to show me where they were sleeping and they took me to their bed. I inspected the blanket on their bed, it was not ours but at least it kept them warm at night.

'How are the women treating you?' I asked Max.

'They're okay,' he said, 'but we're not allowed to make any noise as we're close to the watchtower.'

Jacky, who had not spoken a lot, suddenly said, 'Do you think we'll see Mum and Dad again one day?'

'Of course, darling.'

I put my arm around him. For a while we talked and then I really had to go. I waved to all the children and walked towards the door. By now I had found out that the short woman was called Luba and the other Hermina. When I opened the door to leave, Sister Luba came over and asked for my name.

'Hetty,' I told her. 'Can I come back tomorrow?' I asked in broken German, at the same time using my hand, pointing at myself and making a movement towards the room. Sister Luba understood me and said yes.

I walked slowly back to my room. It was late in the afternoon. It was not cold, or at least I did not feel it. I was so happy that I was allowed to see Max and Jacky and all the children. I was not so happy that the women had used our blankets to shut off their sleeping quarters. But what could I do about it?

While all these thoughts had been going through my

mind, I had nearly covered the distance back to the barracks. I hadn't met anyone on the road. It was a great improvement on our old camp, as that had become so overcrowded. What was even better was there was no rollcall.

Eva was already back in our room. She was happy to see me. 'Where have you been?' she asked.

'I've been to see the children. They're all right. How did you go today? Did you get us something to eat?'

'No,' Eva said. 'I've taken two biscuits, I was so hungry.'

'So am I,' I said, climbing up.

Silently Eva watched me as I ate two small biscuits.

'Things are looking grim,' I said. 'There are only about three biscuits left. What are we going to do?'

'I don't know. I hope they won't let us starve to death. I found out that the women in the barracks near the hospital don't have food either,' Eva said.

We were both silent, busy with our own thoughts.

'We'd better go to sleep,' I said. 'When we sleep, we don't feel so hungry.'

When I woke up the next morning, Eva and Bram had gone. I put on my coat before I went outside and took a red scarf as well, which I tied around my head to keep my ears warm.

My stomach was empty and hurt at times, reminding me that for the last couple of days I'd had almost nothing to eat. The water from the tap was very cold. My hands felt like iceblocks after I had washed them and splashed my face with water. I went back to the room and found the jar of sugar. I took one teaspoon of sugar and hid the jar under my clothing in the suitcase again.

The time went by slowly. After a few hours, I could stand it no longer and decided to see the children. It was still early in the morning.

I walked towards the children's barrack. When I arrived, I knocked at the window. A little girl opened the door for me. I entered, a little apprehensively. Sister Luba was occupied with Phillipje and Sister Hermina was tidying up. I noticed that some of the children had no shoes on, and some little ones no pants. Automatically, I started to dress the little ones and put on shoes and socks where needed. I organised a few of the children to do some of the chores they had done earlier, such as straightening their beds, picking up discarded or dirty clothing and putting them in a heap to be sorted out later. Max and Jacky were very happy I was there, and they helped to achieve some order in the room.

Iesy was in bed with a sore throat. His eyes were shining and he had a fever. He'd caught a cold, so I told him to stay in bed to keep warm. Poor Iesy, he was a sorry sight.

After a few hours I realised that no one had had anything to eat. I asked Sister Luba if she had any food for the children and she told me Lady Doctor had gone out to see if this could be organised.

I returned to the children and told them to be patient and sit around the table in readiness. I joined them at the table and kept them busy by playing simple games and telling them a story, but as time ticked by their attention waned and I could see them becoming very lethargic.

I asked Sister Luba's permission for the children to play outside for a while so they could get some fresh air. I went outside with them. As we walked around the area in front of the barrack, the boys and girls were running around, glad to be outside for the first time in three days.

After about twenty minutes, I told everybody to go back inside and put their coats away. When we entered, Sister Luba told us to sit at the tables. I realised that while we were outside, the doctor had brought us some food.

After I had organised the children around the table, I made a move to leave. I felt I had no right to stay to share their food as I did not belong with them, although I was very, very hungry. I said goodbye to the children and hugged Max and Jacky before I walked towards the door.

Before I reached the door Sister Luba waylaid me. 'Don't you want to eat?' she asked.

I hesitated. 'But it's your food.'

Sister Luba took my arm and guided me back to the chair I had vacated. 'Sit,' she said.

The children were delighted to have me back to share some of the food with them. I felt embarrassed but also very happy. I had only had a few biscuits to eat in the past three days.

The meal didn't take long. Each child got a slice of brown bread with jam and a beaker of warm tea. Slowly I ate my bread, trying not to upset my stomach. My stomach played tricks on me. After it had been empty for so long, it did not want to accept food when I ate something quickly.

When we were all finished and the table was cleaned, I decided to go back to my room and rest. I felt very tired all of a sudden. I said my farewells to Max and Jacky and told them I'd be back in the morning.

I slept right through the night and woke up at first light. I hadn't heard Bram and Eva return. They were both still asleep. I wondered what they were doing all day. I knew what I was going to do. As soon as possible, I would go to the children. And I did.

I went to the children about mid-morning and helped with the chores as I had done the day before. When it was time to eat, it was natural that I also got my share. At times during the day I had caught Sister Luba watching me, but she never said anything to me. I was still scared of her, and I kept my distance as much as possible. But when I was about to leave, she stopped me at the door and asked me if I knew where she could get some sugar. Through her connections in the kitchen she wanted to have a cake baked for Lady Doctor, whose birthday it was the next day.

I wondered which child had blabbed. Somebody must have told her about my sugar. What should I do? My brothers' lives depended on this woman. I made a snap decision.

'I have some sugar,' I told Sister Luba. 'I'll bring it to you.'

I walked quickly to my room, cursing the one who had given the information away. I took a full jar out of the suitcase and hid it under my coat, holding it with one hand. I walked back, hoping that nobody would notice the treasure I was carrying. I was aware how vulnerable I was to a robbery attempt, but my return to the children's barrack went uneventfully.

When I entered, Sister Luba was at the door and invited me into the private area where she and Lady Doctor were sleeping. Once inside, I pulled the jar from under my coat. Sister Luba produced a white cup from somewhere. I opened the lid of the jar and poured the sugar into the cup. When the cup was half-full I slowed the flow of sugar with the intention of stopping, but Sister Luba pushed the rim of the cup onto the jar, indicating that she wanted more. With a bleeding heart, I saw the volume of sugar decrease in the jar, as more and more sugar poured into the cup. When the cup was nearly full, Sister Luba indicated that was enough. I stopped and screwed the lid on tight. There was only a third of the sugar left in the jar.

Sister Luba asked me what I wanted in exchange for the sugar.

'Nothing. Just be good to my brothers,' I said.

She looked at me with disbelief when I said that I didn't want anything in return. She thanked me profusely and said that she would tell the doctor that I had given her the sugar.

Before I left I went to see Max and Jacky and gave them each a spoonful of sugar to eat. I also gave Iesy a teaspoon of sugar as he was still sick in bed. He had seen me give the sugar to Max and Jacky and my conscience wouldn't allow me not to let him share a little bit.

The next day, when I arrived to see the children in the morning, Sister Luba called me into her private cubicle. She showed me a plate with three small cakes and said she would divide them between the children. Later in the afternoon she gave each child a minuscule piece of cake. It was so lovely, even though it was so small, but it wasn't enough to still our hunger. In the past few days, there seemed to have been a problem obtaining food for the children. We had been spoilt before, with potato soup and rice, but no food had arrived for us recently except for some loaves of bread, and we received only half a slice of bread for our meal during the day. The children became listless again and a lot of them came down with heavy colds.

The weather had become colder and there was no heating in the room. Max had to stay in bed for two days with a high fever. I found some aspirin in my suitcase and gave them to him, which soon reduced the fever. We wore nearly all the clothes we possessed to keep warm inside the room: two jumpers, double socks and overcoats. I kept my red silk headscarf on day and night to keep my ears warm.

The food supply dwindled until one morning a few boxes of big carrots arrived. The raw carrots were horrible but at least we could fill our stomachs with something. My jaws ached from trying to chew the carrot pieces, which then cramped my empty stomach. I had to choose between going hungry and being in pain. I chose the former. Every day I gave Max and Jacky a teaspoon of sugar from the small jar I carried in my coat pocket.

I had become a regular part of the group of children, staying with them all day and only going to my barrack to sleep. I hadn't seen much of Eva and Bram lately but I did not care. Our barrack was on the edge of the concentration camp, far removed from the misery in the other sections. Our section was quiet and no atrocities took place. You hardly ever saw anyone outside the hospital and no sound could be heard coming from within. I had no inclination to investigate inside the hospital, and always hurried past it on my way to and from the children's barrack.

Christmas had gone and it was New Year — the first day of 1945. I knew this because the guard who patrolled the camp with two ferocious-looking dogs had called out his New Year greetings to the guards in the watchtower. What would the future hold for us? Perhaps this year we would be freed. Hope rekindled in my heart and I sent up a prayer while I walked towards the children's barrack. I spoke to my mum and my dad, hoping that they would be able to hear me.

That morning I asked the children to sing with me. We sang all the simple songs we had learned at school. When one song was finished, somebody would start on another one and we all joined in. It was the first time I saw Sister Luba smile, and when we were out of breath and our strength gone, she and Sister Hermina sang two beautiful Russian songs.

Chapter 10

On 4 January 1945, early in the morning, all hell broke loose in our section of the camp. We could hear screaming and running feet. Our door was forcibly opened and a female SS guard screamed, 'Everyone out and bring your luggage!' Bram and Eva lost no time in going outside with their suitcase, leaving me alone in the room. There was no way I could carry all the suitcases assembled on my bed. I was desperate and contemplating what I should do when a female guard walked in to inspect the room. I sat on my bed, unable to move. Her eyes met mine and I was sure that her whip would land on me, but for some reason she made out that she hadn't seen me. As she turned towards the door to leave, another guard entered and started to talk very animatedly. As if it were a dream, I could see the first guard was manoeuvring her position so that the second one had her back to me. Slowly I slithered under my blanket, trying to make myself invisible. Then one of the children, Maxy K, walked in, calling out my name at the top of his voice. He walked straight past the two guards towards my bed. There was no way out. I had to sit up. With one eye on the two guards I asked Maxy what he wanted.

'You have to come at once to Sister Luba,' he said.

'Why? Are you sure it is me?' I still did not trust Sister Luba.

'Yes,' Maxy said. She told me to get the girl with the red headscarf. You must come now!'

With a bouncing heart I slid down from the bed. Maxy was pulling on the sleeve of my coat and for a moment I hesitated to walk past the two guards. I mustered all my courage and swiftly walked past them while they were still in conversation. I sighed with relief when Maxy and I reached the outside, and we ran all the way towards the children's barracks. When we ran past the hospital, we could see the sick people being herded outside, accompanied by yelling and the use of the whips. I recognised a woman who was the wife of a business associate of my father. They were being lined up by the kapos.

When Maxy and I arrived at the children's barracks, Sister Luba and Lady Doctor were standing at the door. Sister Luba told me that our camp was being evacuated, but the children were allowed to stay. Lady Doctor wanted to ask Commandant Kramer if I could live with the children. She took my hand and we walked back to the area where the sick people were being lined up. As we came closer, I could see a tall man dressed in a black uniform standing alone. He was immaculately groomed, his jet-black hair was combed back and his black boots were so shiny that the light reflected off them. We stopped at a respectful distance away from him and stood mouse-still. If he noticed our approach, he gave no inkling of it.

While we were waiting to be noticed, I had the opportunity to observe him. His hair was cut short at the back, he had a fat neck like a bulldog, and he constantly hit one of his boots with a short whip. He stood there like Caesar, overseeing the lining up of the sick people. To impress the Commandant, the guards and kapos acted more cruelly towards the poor creatures.

Lady Doctor and I remained still, not moving a muscle. The minutes felt like hours, until Commandant Kramer turned towards us. He spoke one word to the doctor, ignoring me. *'Jawohl!'* The word was a command which stood no nonsense.

'Sir, may I take the little one with me as well?' the doctor asked.

Only then did he turn his eyes to me and so I came face to face with the Beast of Belsen. Evil authority showed on his arrogant face. He had black bushy eyebrows and dark brown piercing eyes, which inspected me from top to toe. After he had scrutinised me, he nodded his approval to the doctor and barked, *'Los!'*

Before he could change his mind, the doctor and I ran for our lives back to the children and Sister Luba. When Lady Doctor told Sister Luba that I could stay, she put her arms around me and said, 'I have now paid for the sugar.'

That cup of sugar saved my life.

In the afternoon, when peace was restored in our section of the camp, I went back to my old room with a small group of children and Sister Hermina, and we carried all the suitcases which had been stored on my bed to the children's barracks. I handed over everything except my own suitcase to Sister Luba. I also kept my blanket which I put on the bed I would share with Max. How happy everybody was that I now belonged to the Children's House of Belsen.

Life started to fall into a routine in the Children's House. As soon as I woke up in the morning I helped the little ones to get dressed warmly. In fact, we were all dressed up as if we were outside. It was bitterly cold and fresh snow had fallen soon after the New Year. As I looked through the fence, the world outside the camp was white as far as the eyes could see, with no sign of life. The air was crisp and clear in the mornings when I took the children outside. It was never more than ten minutes before the cold became too much for us. When we came back inside we huddled together to keep warm. The hours dragged and boredom set in. The children became lethargic. There was very little to eat.

Our barrack was the only occupied building in this section of Belsen, right at the very end of the camp along the fenced perimeter. The doctor moved somewhere closer to the SS camp, and whatever her support had been when she slept in our barracks, this disappeared when she left. Sister Luba had to find us food every day. Some days she would be away for hours; sometimes she returned without any, other times she brought us beautiful potato soup and bread. We were so far away from the main part of the camp that the kitchen forgot to cater for us. Things started to look pretty bleak when we had to live on one thin slice of bread for the whole day.

Sister Luba left early in the morning to get food. In the meantime Sister Hermina looked after the two babies and I looked after the smaller children. Iesy, Max and Jacky and a few other children were still sick. I gave Max and Jacky a spoonful of sugar when no one was around, so they would have some energy to fight the cold.

A strong bond grew between Iesy and myself. As the oldest of the children we started to discuss our problems and tried to solve them as well as we could. The very first time I had encountered Iesy was in Amsterdam, in Christmas 1942. I had gone with Max and Jacky to a small theatre to see an amateur play, *Aladdin's Wonderful Lamp*. Iesy played the role of the king's evil adviser like a born actor. I was very impressed. Now, as I stood next to his bed in Belsen, I told him how much I had enjoyed

Aladdin and the part he had played. I suggested that we organise a play for the children.

Two days later Iesy was able to get out of bed, and we started to make a plan to entertain the children. I had been in school plays, although it seemed like a hundred years ago. Soon some of the children became aware of the pending entertainment and their spirits lifted in anticipation. Their lethargy disappeared and they were distracted from their hunger pains. A proper play was out of the question, even a variety show was too much, so Iesy said, 'Let's put the tables together to make a stage and we'll go from there.'

Willing hands put the tables together, and in a short time the chairs were arranged in rows in front. Iesy climbed onto the tables and told everybody to sit down, including Sister Hermina and the helpers, Sister Hella and her mother.

Iesy started to sing. His voice was not schooled but soon everybody was singing along with tunes from happier times in Holland. After about an hour we all were exhausted, but everyone agreed that it had been a nice show.

After two weeks of misery, existing on hardly anything to eat in the unbearable cold, Sister Luba told us that we had to move to another part of Belsen. She had organised about ten helpers to assist with the children and the luggage. Early in the morning they left with most of the children, and I was left behind with a few children, guarding some of our small possessions. Dusk had arrived when Sister Hermina and some of the helpers returned to fetch us. It was about time! We had had nothing more than a raw carrot to eat for the whole day. There was nothing to drink, not even water, and it had been a trying experience looking after the little ones on my own.

Sister Hermina carried a little girl, and I held on tightly to two other little ones as we walked back over the long main road which divided the camp in two. After we had passed the vegetable kitchen where Mum used to work, Sister Hermina motioned for us to turn left, and there behind the kitchen was a gate in the fence. As we came closer, a woman prisoner opened the gate and let us in. Sister Hermina said something to her in Polish as we filed past. Darkness was falling quickly now and we hurried the rest of the way. I noticed a dark-looking building on the left of the road which showed no signs of life. The door stood wide open but we could see nothing inside. About ten minutes later, we went through the gates into a compound and entered our new barracks.

Sister Luba and her helpers had created a dormitory and a room where we could eat. How she had managed it, I do not know. The beds were two-storey bunks and the room looked very clean. All the beds had been made in readiness for the night. The children who had arrived earlier during the day were very happy to see me and showed me my bed. It was the top bunk in the far left corner of the room in front of the window. A double row of beds stood in the middle and one more row along the opposite wall. I shared my bed with Phoebe, a nice girl who used to live not far from us in Amsterdam. At the end of the bed, mounted on the wall, were two wooden shelves with a small curtain over them. I put my meagre belongings into the locker. I still had some sugar left and some tea in a blue tin. I hid both under the remnants of my clothing.

We all slept very soundly that night. Two women kept watch over us during the night, and a light at the far end of the room was on during the dark hours. Sister Luba had organised it well and after a few days we all felt at home.

I did not have to dress the little ones now as the helpers did this in the morning, and most of us went to bed fully dressed anyway. To keep warm was of prime importance. If we smelt bad, we did not notice it. We had become used to it, I suppose.

We had strict instructions not to leave the compound and to make sure we did not leave, Sister Luba posted a helper on the gate who stopped anyone from leaving or entering without permission.

Seated around a long table each morning we would be given a half slice of bread with jam and a beaker of tea or water. Our food rations had become more regular as we were incorporated into the hospital section and no longer on the outskirts of the camp. When breakfast was over, the children were allowed to play outside within the compound. The end of the dormitory had about eight empty bunks, so it soon became the headquarters for Iesy, Max, Jacky, Louky, Maurice, Gerry and me. We would sit on top of the beds for hours and talk about Amsterdam and our families, but most of all about food. The yearning for good, wholesome, life-sustaining food was felt by all of us as a constant pain.

When we squatted on top of the bunks it was usual for Iesy to do most of the talking. His imagination knew no bounds. He told us about the Portuguese synagogue in Amsterdam, which he said was under protection from the Germans as a monument. I could recall the German guards outside the synagogue but I had believed that this was to prevent the Portuguese Jews from going to their services. He told us how he had attended the services on Friday night with his father and uncle, and the deep satisfaction he got from his religion.

One morning Iesy told us that the building further up the road from our new home was the morgue.

'How do you know that?' Max asked. 'Have you been outside the gate?'

'I sneaked out when there was no one on the gate,' Iesy said. 'Anyway, that's where they bring the dead bodies.'

That was the building I had noticed the night Sister Hermina brought me down from the old barrack. No wonder I felt funny when we passed it.

'I've been thinking that if the SS are going to kill us I'm not going to stand still to let them do it. I'm going to run away,' Iesy said.

'Where to?' Louky asked.

'I don't know, but I'm not going to let them put me in the morgue,' Iesy replied.

No one spoke as we contemplated the horrible fate Iesy had portrayed. After a short time Gerry and Jacky said they would also run if they could. I said nothing. Where would we run to? There was no way out. That night I had nightmares where the SS chased me relentlessly through the camp.

The days became weeks and the cold weather did not let up. We were indeed very lucky that we did not have to attend rollcall. The morgue just up the road was full and the bodies started to pile up outside the building. From our compound you could just see it. The mound became bigger and bigger as the freezing days went by.

Life in our new barrack became more organised. One of the helpers, Sister Hella, was a beautiful young Polish woman with golden hair. Her mother was also a helper, a small, scrawny woman with sharp features and a scarf constantly around her head. She was assigned to keep the floor in the dining room clean, so she always held a broom in her hand. She was not a friendly person, and when the children sometimes wanted to warm their hands near the stove burning in the middle of the room, she would shout, 'Go away from the stove,' and threaten the children with the broom. When this happened, the children would run to me for protection, complaining that 'the Witch' would not allow them near the stove to get warm. I told them to be good and stay clear of the stove as it was reasonably warm in the dining room. Usually I told them to sit around the table and I would tell them a story. I had the respect of all the children and they accepted my guidance. They came to me with their worries and problems. Young and old understood without being taught that we had to stick together and help each other in order to survive.

Sister Luba had dark brown eyes and a small mouth. Her eyes, although demanding, were kind, but when she was angry her mouth would set in a narrow line and God help those who got the lash of her tongue. When she was not in a good mood, we stayed out of her way. Sometimes she returned empty-handed, only to go back to the kitchen a few hours later. When this was the case, Sister Luba usually took Iesy and Max with her, or at other times, Iesy and Louky, in an effort to attract pity for the little ones in her quest for food.

The first few weeks of the new year were good for us. Sister Luba was able to get food for us in the morning and in the afternoon. How wonderful it was to have breakfast, sometimes with porridge or rice, and another meal at night! We who had gone hungry for ten long months in the Sternlager where we lived on carrots and parsnips

The Children's House, Barrack 211.

(Courtesy of the British Imperial War Archives)

floating in brown warm water, could not believe our luck. The hollow cheeks of the children started to fill out a bit and at times laughter was heard. But time still dragged.

The mild weather over Christmas and New Year changed and snow blanketed the entire camp, with temperatures far below zero. Although the Children's House was isolated from the main camp, news of immense brutality and suffering filtered through to our barrack. We heard of prisoners standing on rollcall for hours on end in this freezing weather. We knew all too well what it meant, as we had shared the same experience many times in the Sternlager. Thanks to Sister Luba, we did not have to stand on rollcall. We were counted in the barracks by two of Sister Luba's helpers.

Then, one very cold and windy afternoon in about the third week of January, we were told to come to rollcall in the open area. It was in front of a two-storey wooden house surrounded by trees. We dressed as warmly as possible, remembering that rollcall could last for many hours. Everybody who was lodged in our barrack, number 211, had to be present, including the babies, the sick and the helpers.

The wind was howling through the trees as we stood huddled together, shivering with cold. Inhabitants from other barracks were standing nearby. They had been there long before us. We waited. It became clear that this was not a 'usual' rollcall where we had to line up in rows of five and stand to attention. It had been called to register every person in this part of camp. After about an hour it was our turn. By now the other groups had left for their respective barracks.

While we were waiting we were told that this registration was being done in order to have a number tattooed on our forearm. One by one we were ordered to come forward towards administrators sitting at trestle tables, watched by female guards. When my turn came I went forward with Jacky and Max beside me. A hard-faced woman asked for my name, date of birth and the city from which I had come. After she wrote all this information on a sheet of paper she told me that my number from that moment on was 10564. Until I was tattooed, I had to have 'No. 10564' written on some white cloth and sewn on the front of my coat or jumper. My coat had to have a red stripe painted on the back to indicate I was a prisoner. The coat would be collected at a later date so that the red stripe could be painted on it. The whole miserable exercise distressed the children enormously. They were all terrified about being tattooed.

The administrators made good progress with the older children, who knew their names, but when the little ones, from babies to five-year-olds, had to supply this information, the persistent questions started them crying, and the older children were not allowed to come to their assistance. The administrators realised they were getting nowhere and, after some consultation with the female guards, our group was allowed to return to our barrack, after standing in the freezing cold for more than three hours. Sister Luba was instructed to make up the list with the help of the older children to be collected in a few days' time. Mercifully, there were no more rollcalls.

It was about the last week in January when Sister Luba told me to accompany her on one of her trips for food. We left after eight o'clock and walked the entire length of the camp. Then we took the great dividing road through the SS section, and as we neared the gate to the entrance of the concentration camp, there was a guardhouse with three SS guards inside, just as I remembered it from when I first came to Bergen-Belsen.

Sister Luba gave her number, which had been tattooed on her arm in Auschwitz, and explained our mission. She smiled at the guard and he responded with a friendly face and told her she could enter the camp with *die Kleine* — this being me. It was apparent that Sister Luba had a magic smile to which the SS guards responded favourably, and that they knew about her work at the Children's House. Sister Luba had taken us into her care nearly two months before, and on some days she had to come through this gate twice to obtain food for us from the kitchens. What courage this little woman had, to mesmerise these evil men.

'*Danke*,' Sister Luba said, pulling me away from the guardhouse after she received permission to go through.

She held my hand firmly in hers as we walked into the main camp and towards the food storage place. When we arrived at the store, I saw two women I remembered from the Sternlager who worked in the store. They were very surprised to see me and asked a lot of questions. While we were talking, Fritz, the Scharführer in charge of the food store, came over, and the women explained to Fritz that I was one of the 'orphans' left behind on St Nicholas' night. Fritz turned to one of the women and told her to get me a salami. As she gave it to me she said, 'Cover it with your coat so no one can see it.'

In the meantime, the other woman returned with a second salami. 'Here,' she said, 'take this one too. Quickly, cover it up before the guard sees it.'

I took the second salami from her but I had a problem holding onto them under my overcoat. They were quite heavy and I wasn't strong, but I was determined to get them back to the children. Sister Luba couldn't help me to carry them as she wasn't wearing an overcoat. In the freezing cold she was still wearing a blue cotton blouse with short sleeves and a black skirt.

I struggled the long, long way back to our barracks while the weight of the salamis became heavier and heavier. I was exhausted, but rewarded by the smiling faces of the children when they were told they would be given bread with salami for dinner.

After this experience I decided there must be an easier

way of carrying a salami without detection. A few days later I had an idea. The slacks that Sonja had sent me had very wide legs, so I cut open the bottom of the pockets and extended their lengths by sewing one of my father's socks on the end of it. This created pockets about the length of a salami. By sliding the salami (if I ever managed to get another one) into the long pocket it could hang unseen inside my slacks. As it was such a perfect hiding place, I also sewed whatever spare socks I could find into Max, Jacky, Iesy and Louky's pants.

Chapter 11

Sister Luba was now well known in the camp as our protector. She had gathered around her a group of women who were all dedicated to her work. There was no doubt that Sister Luba was the driving force, while Sister Hermina was second in charge and took command when Sister Luba was away on her food-finding efforts.

Our whole life centred around Sister Luba. She gave us the security we so desperately needed. She always left early in the morning to organise food for us, and the children would wait at the gate of our compound for her return. When they spotted her coming down the road they would run into the barrack, calling out, 'Sister Luba is coming, Sister Luba is coming!'

One night when we all were in bed, we heard many footsteps in the corridor of our barrack. I decided to investigate what was going on. When I cautiously opened the door of our dormitory I saw a few prisoners carting stacks of bread loaves into Sister Luba's room. When I went to the door of the room I could see hundreds of loaves. Sister Luba saw me and she put a finger to her lips, silently telling me not to ask questions. When the prisoners left, she told me that a young SS officer had helped to organise the bread for the children.

The next day the SS officer came to our barracks. Our benefactor was young, perhaps twenty-five, and his name was Maximillian. It soon became apparent that he had taken a liking to Sister Hella. He made many visits to our barracks, mostly at night, when he had organised bread or flour to be delivered.

It was about the second week in February 1945 when I heard wailing coming from the dining room. I ran towards the noise as quickly as my legs would carry me. In the dining room Sister Luba and two other sisters were crying.

'What has happened?' I asked no one in particular.

No one answered and the commotion became worse as the children started to cry from fright and bewilderment at seeing Sister Luba behave in such an unusual way. After about fifteen minutes the noise subsided and Sister Luba saw me standing with the children. What a sight she was, her face streaked with tears and her eyes red and swollen. This frightened me and when I went to her she put her head onto my shoulder and cried.

'Oh God, Phillipje is dead,' she kept saying.

I went numb with shock. I knew that baby Phillipje was sick because Lady Doctor had come to our barrack with

Kurt, the SS doctor a few days ago. I had seen them examine Phillipje and then move him to the hospital for a middle ear operation. Phillipje was returned to our dormitory about eight o'clock that night. The day before it had looked as if he was making a good recovery, and now he was dead. I felt a deep sorrow in my heart. I wondered if Phillipje had possessed the will to live. He had been such a quiet baby. Unless propped up, he would not sit up by himself. He had seldom cried. I believed that Phillipje was missing his mother so much that he did not want to live. Of course, the poor baby never had the nourishment needed to grow. I was crying now with the rest.

When things quietened down, Sister Luba told Sister Hermina to help her take Phillipje away to the morgue. They both went to the dormitory and I followed but stayed at a distance from Phillipje's bed. I saw Sister Luba very gently roll Phillipje in a blue baby blanket. Sister Hermina picked up the small bundle and, with Sister Luba following her and crying all the time, they passed me on the way out. I had a glimpse of the blue bundle but it felt unreal. It was as if Phillipje was not in the blanket at all. Maybe his little soul had already left his body and was now searching for his mother.

'Rest in peace,' I murmured as Sister Luba and Sister Hermina left the barrack for the morgue.

It was the first death within our group and our spirits were very low during the next few days.

One night, three Polish children arrived from Ravensbrück. Their heads were shaven but they looked healthy. They were the first children of a different nationality to join our group: two girls and a boy. The oldest girl, Mala, was about the same age as me. We couldn't communicate with them so they stayed in the dining room where they could talk to Sister Hermina, Sister Hella and the Witch.

Because of the bad weather all the children were confined to barracks, making the dormitory and dining room very crowded. Yet no one argued with each other or squabbled. We all knew that in order to survive, we had to be good to each other. Within all this misery, somehow we developed a solidarity and commitment to each other other. There was nothing to do, so most of the children were hanging around or lying on their beds. We were very bored. As I looked around the dormitory, it occurred to me that this was not good. Our minds had to stay active in order to stay healthy. One of the girls, Leni, was already very sick and did not move from her bed now. Some of the children were always standing near her bed, talking to her to cheer her up. Leni was a lovely girl, who never complained and always spoke to you with a friendly smile. We had no way to make her better, no matter how much we loved her.

I realised something had to be done and I suggested to Iesy that we should make another attempt to put on some sort of show for the children. Iesy agreed to give it another go, and I told the children in the dormitory about the plan. Magically, the lethargy disappeared and everybody had ideas. I intended to do a rhythmic dance I had learned in Amsterdam during gymnastics. Because we had no music, a few of the children had to sing 'The Blue Danube'. We started rehearsing in the dormitory. It sounded terrible at first, but after a few false starts they got the hang of it. I rehearsed the dance as well as I could, while Iesy organised some sketches with a few older boys. We were very serious about it all, and, most importantly, it gave us something to do, and took away the boredom.

The day of the show arrived. Just like our previous show we put all the tables in the dining room together for the stage. With the help of a few Sisters we were able to string a rope across the room to hold up two blankets, which served as stage curtains. Four boys were nominated to open and close the curtains as required. Every chair was taken in our improvised theatre, and when the curtains opened I could not believe my eyes, as there in the first row was the camp elder, Frau Stana, and four female guards. I whispered to the 'actors' to do their very best so we would not embarrass Sister Luba. Then I was on. While the children sang 'Die Danube so blau so blau so blau', I performed the routine I had danced so many times in Amsterdam.

The show lasted an hour and was a great success. Of course, we were very clumsy at times with no props or costumes, but the audience applauded at the right times.

When the show was nearing its end the guards left with the camp elder. Sister Luba accompanied them to the door and let out a big sigh of relief when they had gone. She lost no time in telling us how proud she was of us, and we could see that she was happy that everything had turned out so well.

The success of the show resulted in the female guards becoming more aware of the Children's House. A few days afterwards, two guards entered our dormitory in the afternoon. All the children in the room stopped whatever they were doing and nobody spoke. No one moved a muscle as they slowly walked among us. One guard took a liking to Max and asked for his name in a friendly way. Although Max was very skinny, he was still good-looking with his black hair and blue eyes.

The guard started a conversation with Max while I watched them from the top of my bunk. She told Max that she had seen the show and was sorry that we had no music. Max agreed with her and said, 'If I had a mouth organ I could play it.'

'I will get you a mouth organ,' she told Max.

After the guards left, Max came over to me. 'Did you hear, Hetty? She's going to get me a mouth organ,' he said.

'I wouldn't get your hopes too high, Max. You can't trust them,' I said.

The amazing part about this encounter was that Max had

spoken in Dutch and the guard had spoken in German, yet they both seemed to have understood each other.

Two days later the same guards walked into the dormitory in the afternoon. One of them was Hilde, the one who liked Max. She sought him out immediately and handed him a small parcel. When he opened it there were two pairs of socks and, unbelievably, a beautiful mouth organ. Max's whole face radiated with happiness. Soon he was able to extract a simple tune from the organ, and the guard smiled as she watched him while she sat opposite Leni's bed on the lower bunk. As usual I was sitting on top of my bed and observed the scene from above. Was it really possible that a SS woman could have a heart? No, I decided, I will be on guard as I do not trust them. I called Max to my bed and I whispered to be careful. He nodded. Because Max had received a gift, the other children came closer to Hilde, who appeared to enjoy the attention. When the guards left, they told us they would soon be back.

Obtaining food became difficult during the month of February 1945, and Sister Luba had a hard time getting enough for us. It was bitterly cold and when she returned from a fruitless journey, she often became despondent. At these times I noticed that the Witch was really a good woman. She would remove Sister Luba's boots, massage her tired feet and order Sister Hella to get a dish of hot water so she could bathe Sister Luba's feet. I watched

Sister Luba relax and regain her strength while she poured her heart out in Polish to the Witch, who, in a gentle voice, would calm her down until she was ready to go out again.

After one such occasion Sister Luba wanted me to accompany her to look for food. As we had done many times before, we walked the long way through the camp to the kitchen. This time we targeted the kitchen that supplied the men's camp. A Polish kapo was in charge. Sister Luba talked to this man, her face lit up with a dazzling smile. I could not understand exactly what was being said, but I surmised that he told her to wait and be patient for a while.

At that moment the Scharführer came running down from the far end of the kitchen calling out that he had cut himself with a knife. Sister Luba sprang into action, telling the Scharführer that she was a nurse. He told her to follow him into his office so she could give him first aid. I was left standing near the entrance of the kitchen and from there I could see what was happening inside. The steam of the enormous steel cookers escaped into the kitchen, so it was very hot and hazy. The prisoners worked at high speed and a lot of orders were given, none of which I could understand. I waited, perhaps half an hour, before Sister Luba returned with the Scharführer, whose hand was now bandaged. As they re-entered the kitchen he told the kapo to let Sister Luba have sufficient food for the Children's House, and that from now on she could come back every day to kitchen number one.

Sister Luba was appointed four prisoners to carry the containers with food to the Children's House. From that day on getting food became easier. I heard later that this Polish kapo had quite a liking for Sister Luba and he had even told her that one day when the war was over he would like to marry her.

On 24 February 1945 I turned fifteen. Sister Luba was told it was my birthday by some of the children and in the morning she embraced me and wished me many happy returns.

When I told her I was fifteen, she said, 'Don't disclose your age to the SS as they will classify you as an adult and that could have some unfortunate results. Remember this, Hetty.'

I nodded my head. My knowledge of German was improving by the day.

'Tell me,' Sister Luba said, 'have you got *heath*?' I did not understand what she was saying so she repeated the question. Then in a flash of insight I understood: she wanted to know if my periods had started.

'Yes,' I told her.

She then wanted to know if I still had them now. I shook my head. This seemed to upset her. She took my hand and said, 'Do you want them back? I can get you something from Lady Doctor.'

'Oh, no,' I said in my broken German, 'I do not want that at all.'

I could just imagine the mess it would make for me in these circumstances. Reluctantly, Sister Luba agreed.

That day Sister Luba took me with her to get some food for us. She thought that as it was my birthday, Fritz in the food store might give me a birthday present. She was right. When I returned late that afternoon with Sister Luba, I showed the children the beautiful salami Fritz had given me. I had carried it without difficulty in the big pocket of my slacks. Although the salami had been given to me for my birthday, it never occurred to me to keep it for myself. Everything, no matter who found it or 'organised' it, we all shared alike.

Later that day I was told to come to the dining room. When I arrived I saw that we had visitors, namely, the camp elder, Frau Stana, and her second in charge. Sister Luba appeared tense but managed to smile.

'Hetty, Frau Stana has come to take you for a walk with her, so get your coat and comb your hair,' she said.

Sister Luba warned me with her eyes not to ask any questions. I did as she asked and then returned to the dining room where the two women stood waiting for me. Frau Stana took me by the hand and said, 'Come along' and the three of us left the barrack. Once outside we turned towards the end of the camp. The weather was mild and the sun was shining. We passed das Revier — the sick bay — where you were sent if you were dying. At least this was what that barrack was meant for early in January, but now all the barracks were sick bays and the crematorium could no longer cope.

When we left the Children's House, Frau Stana had asked my name but did not speak to me any more, although she gently held my hand. After a few minutes walk we arrived at the fence near a watchtower. The second in charge called something to the guard. I couldn't follow what she was saying but the guard nodded his approval. The second in charge then produced a key and opened the gate in the fence, and we moved outside the perimeter of the camp. It certainly felt strange to be leaving the camp. After walking about twenty metres, the camp elder sat down on a cluster of heather. She motioned for me to sit near her and then resumed her conversation with her second in charge.

Frau Stana seemed to have completely forgotten that I was present, and I had a good opportunity to observe her. She was a tall woman, her jet-black hair hanging down in curls. Her skin was white and her dark eyes were intelligent. She was a very beautiful woman. How could such a beautiful lady do such a cruel job? I wondered. On the other hand, the second in charge definitely looked the part. She was a tall, strong woman with dark blond hair. She had high cheekbones, pale grey eyes and a cruel looking mouth. Both women were dressed in the chequered skirts of the prominents. They also wore knee-high leather boots. You could see yourself in the leather, it was so shiny. As if she could feel my scrutiny, Frau Stana turned to me and said, 'How old are you, Hetty?'

Sister Luba's warnings went through my head, so I lied and said, 'I turned thirteen today.'

'Oh, it's your birthday today, how nice,' she said.

I nodded. After this short exchange she returned her attention to her second in charge. It was difficult to converse with Frau Stana as she spoke German and Polish, and I could only really speak Dutch.

Left to myself, I examined my surroundings. Behind me, a small red brick building stood in a clearing surrounded by a seven-foot high fence. With a shock I realised that this was the crematorium. It looked empty and no smoke came from the chimney. There were no corpses lying in the clearing around the building. I turned my head away. It depressed me.

I spotted some empty sardine tins lying on the ground so I got up and retrieved two of them. The elder hadn't even noticed that I had walked a few metres away. I started to fill the small tins with sand. Then I selected a few small heather plants from near where I sat and created a miniature decoration. It was nice to create something pretty and delicate among all this misery.

Suddenly Frau Stana remembered my presence and

looked at me. I showed her what I had made and she said, 'Nice.' I handed her one of my creations, saying, 'This is for you.'

She looked at it and after some hesitation she told the second in charge to carry it as we were ready to go. I pointed to the second tin with the plants and asked, 'Sister Luba?' Frau Stana nodded so I picked it up and carefully carried it.

When we arrived at the Children's House, Frau Stana said a friendly goodbye to me, which her eyes told me was sincere. The second in charge was not so friendly: her eyes told me that she was glad to be rid of me. I thanked them both for taking me out and quickly skipped into our barrack to find Sister Luba and give her the plant decoration. She was very happy to see me again. She was worried about why Frau Stana had personally requested that I join her on her walk. That evening she handed me an extra slice of bread as a birthday present, which I promptly shared with Max and Jacky.

We all had a slice of bread and salami that night and the children sang 'Happy Birthday' to me. One of the girls, Erica, came forward with a poem she had written for me in Dutch. It went like this:

> Happy birthday to you.
> I give you this bread without butter as I have none,
> but I am sure you will be able to eat.

I hope that your sixteenth birthday you celebrate
in Amsterdam
with your parents and your two brothers.

Erica handed me her slice of bread — her evening meal — but I would not accept it and told her to eat it herself. The very fact that she wanted to give me her bread showed that I was loved, and that she appreciated my care of her. I gave her a big kiss and all the children clapped their hands.

The next day a parcel was delivered for me from Frau Stana. When I opened it, it contained a grey-and-white chequered skirt and a nice woollen jumper that fitted me perfectly. Sister Luba was beaming, she was so proud of me. I had pulled the heartstrings of the camp elder and this could only help Sister Luba in her quest to get food for us.

Life in the entire camp became unsustainable. The cold weather, the lack of food, the rollcalls and the indescribable overcrowding in the barracks resulted in many deaths. The mountain of dead bodies grew and grew, and when we looked out from our windows the corpses stretched as far as the eye could see. Although the odour of decaying corpses must have been horrific, we could no longer smell it.

For about a month two women had kept watch over us during the night. This had been the case since Phillipje was sick and they had stayed on mainly to look after the toddlers. It was also comforting for the bigger children to wake up in the night, see the low light and hear soft conversation. I experienced this feeling of comfort many times when I woke from a restless sleep. I rarely slept peacefully as my mind was always on the alert for danger during the night.

During the last days of February 1945 we heard through the camp grapevine that some of the men from the diamond transport had returned to Belsen and were in the Häftling camp. Max, Jacky and I wondered if our father had returned, so when the female guards came to see us again, Max asked Hilde if she could find out if our father was in the men's camp. Max called me over and said, 'Hetty, Frau Hilde wants to know more details about Dad. She wants to know his birth date.'

After some hesitation I told her: '21 April 1902.'

Max had already told her Dad's name. She promised she would make inquiries but I could see in her eyes that she was cunning and false, and after she left I told Max to be very careful.

Frau Hilde visited the barracks on her own one afternoon. To the smaller children she was now familiar and they crowded around her. They had no idea of the danger she represented, and I believe she used this method to extract information from the unsuspecting children about Sister Luba. She wanted to know if we had enough to eat.

She told me to sit next to her on the lower bunk, and after I sat down, she turned to me and asked, 'How old are you?"

'Thirteen,' I lied, with Sister Luba's warning still imprinted on my mind.

I do not know if the female guard knew I was lying. It would have been a simple task for her to check the records. It was Max who spared me further questions.

'Frau Hilde,' he said, 'do you think it would be possible to get a cream cake? I would like that very much.'

My God, I thought, what courage to ask for something like this, but Frau Hilde told Max that she would try and then she pulled Max close to her and touched his genitals. Max tried to free himself from her embrace, and seeing our astonishment Frau Hilde quickly released him and got up to leave.

'See you soon,' she told Max and she was gone.

Frau Hilde returned two days later and gave Max a little box. When he opened it he found two cream cakes and a ham and salami sandwich inside. Max handed the box over to me and thanked Frau Hilde for her gift. She patted his head and was gone a few minutes later. The small box with its precious contents was handed to Sister Luba, who cut the cake and the sandwich into minuscule parts so that every child could have a piece. The tiny morsels tasted delicious. I doubt if any of us could have managed to eat a full cream cake as our stomachs were not used to this kind of food.

Before Frau Hilde left, Max had asked her again if she had found out anything about our father and she told him that she was making inquiries. If we had been older and wiser we would have refrained from making such a request to an SS woman as it endangered our father's anonymity within the camp. Max's request to find our father would bring Dad to the attention of the SS which could be fatal, but in our innocence we did not think of this.

The day after my birthday it occurred to me that we did not know when Sister Luba's birthday was, so when she returned from the kitchen I asked her. It took some time to find out, as apparently birthdays in Russia and Poland are defined differently. In Holland our birthday is the day we are born. In Russia and Poland, a birthday is on the person's name date, which means there is a saint or an event after which they have been named. After lots of discussion, we believed that her birthday was on 5 March.

This did not leave me much time to organise something special. In fact, I had just nine days. I decided to consult Inge and Gretel, two Dutch women of German origin who sometimes came to see us. Gretel worked at the SS doctors' dispensary, and was able to get her hands on the medicines Sister Luba needed if any of us were sick.

When Inge and Gretel arrived in the afternoon I told them that I needed their help to get a present for Sister Luba's birthday, something really pretty. I also wanted

Inge to write a poem which I could recite. Inge said she would give it a try and I promised her food. This conversation took place in our compound late in the afternoon out of earshot of any small talkative mouths who might reveal the surprise to Sister Luba. Inge and Gretel did not come back until four days later. On a not-so-white piece of paper, Inge had composed a poem in German for Sister Luba's birthday. She had included all Sister Luba's virtues as I had listed them for her.

After Inge had translated the meaning of certain words so I could understand them all, I was quite happy with the result. I then asked Inge if she had been able to find a present for Sister Luba and she showed me a beautiful black-and-white silk scarf with the Dutch trademark *De Bonnetterie.* I was thrilled that she had been able to find such a thing in Belsen, let alone something from Maison de Bonnetterie in Amsterdam. Only the wealthy could afford this exclusive shop.

'One of the old ladies of the Sternlager had it in her suitcase,' Inge answered.

'How much does she want for it?' I asked.

'One-and-a-half bread loaves,' Inge said.

'And what do you want for the poem?' I asked Inge.

Inge looked at Gretel, then she said, 'We would like half a loaf of bread.'

I pondered over this for a while. There was no doubt about it — I wanted this beautiful shawl for Sister Luba, and the poem was important too.

'Okay, I will get you the two loaves of bread, but it has to be in slices. I cannot get hold of a whole loaf for you,' I told them.

Inge and Gretel agreed to the conditions.

'Now,' I said, 'I believe that one loaf has seventeen slices, correct?'

Inge agreed.

'So two loaves makes thirty-four slices of bread?'

Inge and Gretel nodded.

'I will pay you in two parts, so thirty-four half slices on one night and thirty-four half slices on the second night.'

Inge agreed. With that settled I asked Inge to bring me the completed poem tomorrow so that I could have some time to memorise it before Sister Luba's birthday. Inge promised to come back the next day and to write the poem in block letters, as she had noticed that I could not follow her handwriting very well.

I went back into our barrack and sought out Iesy to tell him about my plan. 'I have to organise two bread loaves to get Sister Luba this beautiful shawl, and to pay Inge and Gretel for the poem,' I said.

Iesy did not answer at once. I could see that he was thinking this would be difficult to achieve. People were killed sometimes for one slice of bread and we had to get thirty-four slices together. Somehow we had to do it. Sister Luba was very special to us.

'The only way I can see how to do it is if each of us gives up half the slice of bread we get for our evening meal for two nights. What do you think about it, Iesy?'

Iesy looked very serious. 'That's a lot to ask. We haven't had much food for the past few days.'

'I know it will be a real sacrifice for all of us but I can't see any other way to achieve it, short of breaking into the storeroom,' I said.

Iesy was quiet for a while and then he suggested that we should ask the others if they would agree. I turned to a few children who had been standing close by and told them to fetch everybody into the dormitory. Soon everybody except for the very small ones were standing around me. I told them about Sister Luba's birthday plans and what was needed from them.

'It's your bread ration and if you don't wish to give away half of it for two nights you don't have to do it,' I said.

But everybody agreed to it, and this act alone showed how much the children loved Sister Luba.

The first night I collected the bread during dinner without the Sister in charge noticing a thing. The next night the children again parted with half their evening ration. Although they were very hungry, their love for Sister Luba was stronger than their hunger. Sister Luba meant everything to us. She was our mother in Belsen, our trust in her by that time had no bounds, our love for her was unconditional. She was the angel who took care of us.

The morning of 5 March 1945 arrived. Early in the morning we washed our faces, cleaned our hands and combed our hair, the older children taking care of the little ones. Everybody was lined up for my final inspection before we left for the dining room. When we entered the room we did not sit down as usual but formed a double row with the little ones up front facing the door. Sister Luba, who had been informed the night before that her presence was required, entered the room and the children sang the Dutch birthday song 'She Will Live Long, Hurrah'. Sister Luba was so surprised and her face lit up in a happy smile. The children had kept this secret well.

After the song we told Sister Luba to sit down in a specially decorated chair and then I recited the poem:

Schwester Luba, the name fits like a glove,
You have all our respect and all of our love,
From early morning till late at night
Not once do you let us out of your sight.
The day has barely begun
And already Sister Luba is on the run.
And where is she off to now?
To the kitchen to fetch our chow.
The children wait, asking when she'll be back,
And what she'll bring today
To fill this and that little stomach.
How happy she is when the day's taking

Include potato soup and bacon.
All take their seats, all are present,
Because eating makes our lives so pleasant.
No gate, no wall,
For Luba nothing is too strong or tall,
For she'll do anything
For the children under her wing.
If one gets sick, many weeks on end
Luba knows no rest until the child is on the mend.
Leni is ill, and now
Luba paces endlessly up and down,
And in the night, when all is still
She is still up to give the child a sweet 'pill'.
Once the children had no shoes —
Schwester Luba organised them, swell.
Our lives are in her hands, we know full well,
And all of us are grateful, big and small.
Much more there isn't to tell:
We wish you joy, health and happiness,
And may freedom come quickly for all of us.

Sister Luba was sitting enthralled in her chair. I went over to her and handed her the present, and I told her of the sacrifice all the children had made so we could buy the silk shawl for her. I then put my arms around her neck and as I kissed her I told her, 'We love you, Sister Luba.' By now Sister Luba and all the other Sisters did not have a dry eye. Then Sister Luba got up and walked down the line of children. She thanked and hugged every one of them and we sat around the table to have our breakfast. Sister Luba didn't go out that day. Instead she sent Sister Hermina, who took Max with her to the kitchen.

It was a happy day, until late in the afternoon when two female guards visited. I was called to the dining room. When I entered I could see Sister Luba talking to the two guards who had their backs towards me. When Sister Luba saw me she took me by the hand and said, 'The guards wish you to recite the verse from this morning,' and she pushed me gently in their direction.

One of the guards was Juana Borgmann, who was feared for her brutality. Every fibre in my body warned me to be careful. These female guards were not the same as the ones who had visited us in the dormitory before. My instinct told me that these two women were evil. Somehow I got up enough courage to recite the poem, but when I came to the last line which said 'And may freedom come quickly for all of us', I hesitated and said instead, 'I wish you a happy birthday from all of us'.

Where in the world I found the words I do not know. I could only speak a few German words. I firmly believe that some power from above formed the words in my brain so I could say them. Sister Luba looked very relieved and the guards told me that it was a very nice verse, but they did not look sincere. I was allowed to return to the dormitory. But that was not the end of it.

Two days later I was again requested to come to the dining room. There I saw Sister Luba with some of her helpers standing in front of a mean-faced SS officer who was seated on a stool. Juana Borgmann and the other female guard who had listened to my verse stood next to the SS officer. Sister Luba's face was flushed and her mouth was pulled in a straight line so I knew something was very wrong. Irma Grese turned to me when I entered and said, 'Übersturmführer Herr Fuchs wants to speak to you.'

She pushed me in the direction of the SS officer. He was a skinny, short man, who wore glasses over his piercing dark eyes. His uniform was black and he carried a short leather whip in his right hand. As he was seated his eyes were at the same level as mine. He stared at me intently and then in a soft voice he asked, 'What is your name?'

'Hetty Werkendam, Herr Übersturmführer.'

'What is your name?' he said again very softly. He stared straight into my eyes. They reminded me of a snake and I started to feel alarmed.

With my heart pounding I said again,'Hetty Werk—'

'Esther, you mean, Esther, not Hetty!' Übersturmführer Fuchs screamed.

I reeled back in shock and whispered, 'Yes, Esther.'

'I have heard that you have made enquiries about your father,' he said.

'Yes, Herr Übersturmführer.'

'And what is your father's name?' he asked. Again he stared into my eyes as if he wanted to hypnotise me.

'My father's name is Maurice Werkendam.'

'So,' he said softly, 'Maurice Werkendam?'

I nodded my head in agreement, but Fuchs exploded in fury. 'Moses you mean, Moses, not Maurice!'

I was shaking with fright, and without turning I could feel that Sister Luba and the other Sisters were also afraid of what could happen to me. Then Fuchs calmed down again. 'How old are you?'

I recalled Sister Luba's warning, but he knew my birth name and my father's birth name so he must have checked the records. If I told him I was thirteen he would know I was lying.

'Fourteen, Herr Übersturmführer,' I answered.

Fuchs looked at the two female guards when he heard my answer, but before he could say anything else Sister Luba came forward and stood beside me.

'Herr Übersturmführer, the little one has special permission from the Commandant to be in the Children's House,' she said, with her dazzling smile.

This was evidently news to Fuchs and after consulting in a low voice with the two guards he told me I could go. Sister Hella pulled me into the next room. I was shaking like a leaf. I burst into tears and pressed my face into her body for protection. Sister Hella held me tight and tried to comfort me. I could hear Fuchs screaming something at Sister Luba which I could not understand. Thank God, Fuchs and his ladies soon left, but not before he ordered Sister Luba and Sister Hermina to wear prisoners' garb in the future, threatening that he would personally punish them if they did not obey.

Sister Luba was furious after they left. 'Who has been informing the SS about the Children's House?' she asked. 'It must be someone in our midst.'

But how could one of us do such a thing? Or could it have been those two female guards who visited the dormitory? They had seemed to pump the children for information. On the other hand there were plenty of people jealous of the position Sister Luba held, and jealousy and hatred of those who were in a more fortunate position in the camp were the order of the day.

Sister Luba was very upset that she was not allowed to wear civilian clothing anymore, as she was now known as a prominent. She soon acquired through her 'connections' a few male jackets in grey-and-white striped material. These were unpicked and together made a fitted sports jacket and skirt. Sister Luba wore her blue blouse to complement the outfit. The first day she wore it I told her how smart she looked. She smiled at me and gave me a big kiss.

Chapter 12

I had gone to the kitchen many times with Sister Luba so I knew the way through the camp and the procedure to pass through the SS checkpoint. One day I decided to go to the food store on my own to see if I could get something extra for Max and Jacky. A group of some twenty Polish and Hungarian children had arrived about a week ago, crowding our dormitory and cutting into our food rations — the SS did not increase our quota. The air held the promise of spring as I set out.

The women's camp was large and the barracks had not been built in straight lines but were scattered at different angles amid wooded areas with large trees. It could not be compared with the Sternlager where the barracks were built in a straight line in a much smaller area. This might have originally been designed as a holiday place, I thought, as I walked over the road which snaked through the camp. And what a holiday place did it turn out to be.

When I passed the morgue I could see the mountain of dead bodies spread over an area about the size of a football field. A short distance away two prisoners were cutting into a corpse. I walked away as fast as I could from this depressing sight. Cannibalism! Despite the many barbaric things I had seen, this shocked me deeply.

I broke into a run to escape this evil sight. After a while I slowed to regain my breath. It was peaceful in this part of the camp. There was no one in sight. I was alone and did not meet another soul. Through the trees I could glimpse the road on which we had arrived in Belsen. It seemed such a long time ago, but it was only a year and two months.

As I neared the SS checkpoint my heart started to pound. This would test whether I was able to wander through the camp or not. As I had done with Sister Luba, I went over to the small building where the SS was monitoring everyone who came and went.

Two SS officers were seated behind a desk at the open window facing the road. I walked up to them. They looked at me and one said, 'Where are you going?'

'I am from the Children's House and I am going to see Herr Fritz at the food store.'

'Have you a number?'

'Yes, 10564.'

'You may go through,' he told me after making a note in a book.

That was easy, I thought, as I walked through the gate.

The food store was just over the road on the left. I was lucky, Fritz was standing at the door when I arrived. I greeted him and asked point-blank, 'Can you please let me have a salami for the Children's House?'

He looked down at me and I gave him my best smile.

'Do you belong to the Children's House?' he said.

'*Jawohl*, Herr Scharführer,' I answered.

He turned around and called to someone in the storehouse to bring him a salami. They called back, 'A small one or a large one?'

For a moment Fritz hesitated, then replied, 'A large one.'

I was left standing alone at the door for what seemed a long time before the store person returned with a large salami and handed it to me. This time I was well prepared to carry it home without it being seen. The salami slid into my father's sock and was undetectable as it hung in the wide leggings of my slacks.

I set off 'home' again. Passing the SS checkpoint I waved from the road and the SS officer waved back, indicating that I could pass through. So far, so good.

I started to hurry as it was getting late in the afternoon and the light was fading already. A grey fog started to drift down and although I could still see the road clearly, the barracks slowly got lost in the mist. I knew I still had to pass the mountain of dead bodies, and other dangers lurked for me if anyone discovered that I was carrying a salami. People were killed for as little as a piece of bread. I started to walk faster but shortage of breath made me slow down again.

Stay calm, I told myself, if you run someone will see

you and know you are scared. I knew that in Belsen you must never show that you are scared, otherwise the stronger ones would take control or kill you. I forced myself not to run. The eerie quiet of the morgue on my left told me I was nearly home. Despite my good intentions, I started to run the last part of the way towards the safety of the Children's House.

When I entered the dormitory all the children were already in the room. Our evening ration had been given out. Max showed me the slice of bread waiting for me on my pillow. I climbed up onto my bed and removed the salami from my pocket. It smelled delicious. I hid it behind my back under the blanket and ate my slice of bread. Someone had got me a cup of water. When I had finished I called Jacky and Max over and showed them the salami.

'Where did you get it?' Max asked.

'From Fritz at the food store,' I said.

The children had grouped around my bed, all wanting to see the beautiful salami. Someone handed me a knife and I told everybody to line up. I cut the salami and handed a small slice to each child, but I gave a bigger slice to Max and Jacky as they were my brothers. Everybody enjoyed the salami as it was salty and peppery and this was what our bodies desperately needed. We had been deprived of salt for such a long time that even this small piece of salami helped to strengthen us a little bit.

In about the middle of March we were told that the Red Cross was to hold an inspection. It was amazing how things changed. Our barrack was cleaned from top to bottom. Sister Luba acquired some more helpers. I helped with inspecting and sorting out the clothing that each child should wear during the Red Cross inspection. If things needed to be mended they were taken to Sister Hella. Dirty clothing was washed. A messenger had arrived from Frau Stana, the camp elder, with strict instructions. We had to be cleanly dressed and appear to be happy. If someone from the Red Cross asked us if we were being treated all right we were to say 'Yes'. If they asked if we had enough to eat we had to say 'Yes'. For the next few days we were constantly told what to do and not do. Sister Hermina told us that on the day we would eat our main meal at lunchtime.

When the day finally arrived the dining room held a feast for the eyes. The long tables were covered with white sheets and every child had a thick slice of white bread with butter put before them. The door opened and three men and one woman entered the dining room. Each had a white band with a Red Cross on the left arm. They were accompanied by Frau Stana, Lady Doctor and other medical staff.

To our great surprise, Mr Weiss also entered with the group. How happy I was to see him again. I sat on the end of the table and we found a chair so that he could sit with us. As it happened, the visit of the Red Cross fell on the Jewish Passover and Mr Weiss read from the prayer book he had brought with him before we started our meal. There was no unleavened bread, but that was not important now — we had life-sustaining white bread. Mr Weiss also carried a large box of chocolates, apparently provided for us by the Red Cross. A woman dressed as a nurse came over to Mr Weiss and took the box from him. She told him that she would distribute the chocolates to the children. I knew this woman. She was the dental nurse who had assisted with my teeth. I did not like her then and I did not like her now.

Mr Weiss asked me lots of questions. Were the Sisters good to us? How did we spend our days? I told him how we lived and, of course, I asked him whether he knew if my father was back in Belsen. Mr Weiss told me that about twenty men from the diamond transport had returned from Mauthausen but he did not know who they were.

'It is difficult to find out,' he said, 'but I'll try.'

The room was overcrowded. The children chatted excitedly. The Red Cross people were talking to Sister Luba and the other Sisters, whose faces were smiling brightly. One of the Red Cross people could speak German. Frau Stana stood near the Red Cross people so as not to miss a word that was spoken.

Then the Red Cross people came over to the table to speak to the children. One of them came to me and asked my name, which he wrote down in a notebook. He then wanted to know if the camp management was good to us, if we got enough to eat and if anyone beat us. I answered 'Yes' to the first two questions and 'No' to the third. The man smiled at me and wrote notes in his book. Then he was called away as the party was leaving to inspect our dormitory and the rest of the barrack.

The door of the dining room opened and Sister Luba returned with Sister Hermina from the inspection. Mr Weiss was told that the party had already left the barrack. Reluctantly he rose, then took hold of both my hands and looked down at me,

'You are a brave girl, Hetty,' he said. 'I will see what I can do to find out about your father and let you know.'

We hated to see Mr Weiss go. I closed my hands more firmly into his but he gently removed them. He had to leave. With a last pat on my head he bade us goodbye and quickly left the room to catch up with the others.

We felt so lonely after he left but we had one consolation: we all had a large piece of chocolate. For once Sister Luba let us keep it to eat it as we liked, but she warned us to go easy as it could make us sick if we ate it all at once. Soon we all returned to the dormitory where we discussed the happenings of the afternoon. The bigger children felt optimistic about the future. It was the first time in many months that we'd had contact with people from outside the camp.

What a show the SS had put on, with the help of all of

us, to deceive the Red Cross. That night we had no dinner but it didn't matter as by then we had eaten most of our chocolate.

The visit from the Red Cross aroused a wild longing to be free. The confines of the barrack pressed into me, so I decided to try my luck once more at the food store. When I sneaked out of our barrack, it was early in the morning and the camp was very still. As I passed the morgue I noticed that the pile of bodies had increased considerably. By now I was used to seeing corpses with their eyes wide open and their mouths stretched in hideous grins. Maybe it was their way of saying that they had been released from the barbaric torture and deprivations of the camp.

I still had a long way to go. I passed barracks with no one in sight. I passed smaller divisions within our camp enclosed with a wire fence like our barrack.

Again no one was at the gate when I left the women's camp. Through the trees I could see the empty bathhouse and next to it the store for clothing and other amenities. Where was everybody? I wondered as I walked down the main street. Then, directly opposite the SS checkpoint, I saw the pitiful crouched figure of a prisoner, no more than a skeleton in grey-striped garb, holding up a large pumpkin. At his feet was a sign that read, 'I stole from you'. I had witnessed many evil things in Belsen, but they did not lessen my pity for this poor creature. His hollow cheeks and dull, deep-sunken eyes shook me to the depths of my soul. As I came closer I could hear the SS shout at the luckless man, 'Hey, keep those arms up, thief!' and I saw him raise the pumpkin a few inches higher. I could feel his pain. That pumpkin in his hand must have felt as though it weighed a ton. I had no idea how long he had been out there, but a man in good condition could not sit in that position holding up a large pumpkin for long. This poor skeleton had so much will to survive that he endured this torture, but how long could he keep it up?

I walked up to the open window, averting my eyes from the prisoner. I gave my number to the SS officer.

'You had better be good if you don't want to be punished like him,' he said.

I nodded and gave him my best smile. I was allowed to pass and soon I arrived at the store, only to be told that Fritz wasn't there. Nor were the two Dutch ladies from the Sternlager. The Polish kapo on duty did not want to give me any food.

'Come back when Fritz is here,' he told me.

How disappointed I was. I had started out on the long walk hoping that perhaps I could get another salami. Reluctantly, I turned to go back to the barracks. As I neared the SS checkpoint, I noticed the poor prisoner was now on his knees, but still holding up the pumpkin.

As before I waved to the officer and he nodded that I could be on my way. I was very upset that I had failed, but I kept telling myself that I would try again soon. Food had been scarce in the past few days. Sometimes Sister Luba came back with no food at all, and our rations were cut to one slice of bread a day, which we received at night.

Without realising it, I had already passed the gate of the women's camp and was getting close to a two-storey house standing in a clearing. I could see a wooden cart, usually used to carry dead bodies, parked in front of a wooden chute suspended from the top-floor window into the cart. As I came closer I could see two prisoners catching bread loaves as they came down the chute, and at the same time repeating the number of each loaf, which was accounted for at the top by other prisoners. I could hear them counting aloud in Polish. On seeing all that bread in the cart I walked over and stood beside the SS Scharführer directing the operation. He scrutinised me for a second and then smiled. My mind was made up. I was going to steal one of those loaves. I did not want to consider the consequences if I failed. I edged closer to the cart and felt the wooden side touching my chest. I moved my legs one step back so there would be room to hide a loaf under my coat. I stood very still next to the Scharführer who took no further notice of me. Two male prisoners faced me from the opposite side of the cart, catching the loaves from the chute and placing them in neat rows in the cart as they counted aloud, repeating the numbers announced from the building. Three men were handling the bread loaves upstairs and two downstairs. Then my opportunity came: the men downstairs disagreed with the man at the top about the number of loaves they had sent down.

'Eighty-nine,' one man said.

'No,' the man opposite me said, 'eighty-seven.'

The man on the window started to argue loudly in Polish. I made out that I was very interested in the argument and lifted my head to look at the men upstairs. I could not understand a word that was being said and neither could the Scharführer. He demanded to know from the men upstairs what the problem was. They told the Scharführer that they had sent down eighty-nine loaves. This resulted in a strong denial from the men on the cart. I knew this was the moment. I kept my head up as if I were looking at the men upstairs. The two men in front of me had turned their backs to me. Together with the Scharführer they looked up to the men at the window. I slowly moved my left arm to get hold of a loaf inside the cart. My hand enclosed the bread and, ever so slowly, I gently lifted the loaf high enough to clear the side of the cart. Except for the movement of my arm, I stood motionless. I brought the loaf down until it was hidden under my coat. I released my breath. The men were still disagreeing about the count while the Scharführer gave them a piece of his mind. I remained a few seconds longer, then slowly took the first careful steps on my way.

The Scharführer was so intensely engaged with the

arguing men that he didn't even look at me when I left. For the first ten metres I expected to hear that my theft had been discovered, but when that didn't happen I quickened my pace, and when the arguing men were out of earshot I ran and did not stop until, out of breath, I arrived at the dormitory.

The children looked up in alarm when I burst through the door, but this soon turned into happy smiles as I held the loaf high above my head and practically danced towards my bed. Not only had I 'organised' a whole loaf of bread but I had also outwitted the SS Scharführer, stealing the bread from under his very nose.

Soon the children had grouped around me, wanting to hear every detail of my escapade. One of them asked me if I had been scared, and it was then that the enormity of my deed sank in. If I had been caught in the act, the punishment would have been severe. I shivered and put the thought out of my mind. But what if the Scharführer remembered that I was from the Children's House? Better to leave no evidence around, so I took the knife, cut the bread into chunks and handed them to all the children around me. Max and Jacky got the biggest. When every crumb was devoured I felt more at ease, and as the hours went by I knew that the missing loaf had not been connected with me.

Overnight the weather changed abruptly. Cold blustery winds and sleety rain swept through the camp, creating more misery for the prisoners. We heard of the long hours the adults endured on rollcall from early morning to late in the afternoon. Without proper clothing and food, many prisoners succumbed during these cruel hours, and when the kapos mercilessly beat them, they were left to die in the mud and slush where they fell.

The weather was so bad the children could not play outside, and the dormitory became a bit crowded. On the bright side, the room temperature was bearable from the heat our bodies radiated. The smell of unwashed bodies and bedding in the dormitory must have been horrendous, but we didn't notice it any more.

Leni, who had been sick since the beginning of February, had not been able to leave her bed for weeks. We kept her company and in turn brought her her daily slice of bread, but the poor girl could hardly eat and was wasting away. She would patiently chew a few bites of bread, but the effort was too much for her at times. Bella, who had the most patience, usually tried to feed Leni each morning. She was allowed, with our blessing, to keep the rest of the bread which Leni could not eat. We wanted to spare Leni any pain. It was pitiful to see how skinny she was, but she never complained.

It was the third week in March when Louky came to tell me that Jacky was very sick. I immediately went to his bed to see for myself. Jacky was dozing but when I called his name he struggled into a sitting position and looked at me with fever-glazed eyes.

'How are you, Jacky?' I inquired.

'I'm not feeling so good,' Jacky said. 'I have this terrible headache. Can you get some water for me?'

'Of course.' I turned to Louky and told him to get a cup of water for Jacky straightaway. I told Jacky to lie down again while I fetched him some aspirin that I still had in my locker. When Jacky was settled down again I went back to my bed. From there, I could keep an eye on Jacky and watch what was happening outside.

The mountain of bodies was growing bigger every day. Food became scarcer. Sister Hella's SS officer, Maximillian, had been able to get us a few large sacks of flour, which were delivered during the night. Sister Hella, Maria and the Witch had been cooking little dumplings during the night so the flour would not be discovered. This had become our only source of food during the past few days. The difficulty was keeping the stove in the dining room going so they could heat the water to boil the flour balls. All the beds in the dormitory were already minus one or two wooden slats, as this was our only source of fuel for the stove. The pan previously used as a toilet had been scrubbed clean and was now used to cook the dumplings.

I decided to have another look at Jacky, so I climbed down from my bed.

At that moment we heard a great tumult in the dining

room. Everyone in the dormitory froze, fearing danger. The door to the dormitory was flung open and in stormed Rau, the Arbeitsführer. His face was contorted and he was foaming at the mouth. He was yelling 'Criminals! Pigs!' and started to hit out at us with a rubber truncheon. With his arm raised above his head he looked me straight in the eyes as he rained down the lashes. In his anger he missed me but poor Louky got it right on the top of his head. I could hear Louky's breath escaping as he reeled under the brutal onslaught. Terror reigned in our dormitory but was over just as suddenly as it had started. Rau had gone. We could hear him screaming down the corridor as he left. For a few seconds no one spoke. We were still terrified. I turned to Louky and asked if he was all right. He looked very pale but managed a weak smile.

The dining room was in chaos. Tables and chairs had been overturned. The stove was burning with its door wide open, with parts of the wooden bed planks poking out. In one corner of the room Sister Hella was lying on her bed with her mother, the Witch, attending her. Hella was a terrible sight. She had big blue swellings near her eyes and her upper arms were covered with weals and bruises, as she had raised her arms to protect her head from the brutal bashing. Maria, who had received only a few blows, was in a much better condition and she was able to tell me what had brought on the wrath of Rau.

Sister Hella had been at the stove pushing down the

planks of wood into the fire when Rau had entered the dining room. There had been no warning of his coming, so he had surprised Sister Hella in the act. We had no tools with which to cut the bed planks so we had to use them in their full lengths, pushing them down as they burned up at the bottom.

The sight of 'German property' burning had outraged Rau, prompting his frenzied attack. But Rau never needed much excuse for such behaviour. He was feared right through the camp for his cruelty. I returned to the dormitory to find everyone recovering from the shock.

Jacky appeared to have slept right through all the commotion. He felt very hot so I placed a wet face washer on his forehead to help ease the fever. I had no idea that Jacky was sick with typhus.

As the days went by, more and more of our children, including myself, came down with this grim disease brought about by the lice and bedbugs. You could not see the bedbugs during the day but at night they bit us, and we would wake in the morning with angry, red, itching weals all over our faces and bodies. I looked at the children and their unwashed hair and faces. I decided to do something about it and told them to go and wash and then meet me at the entrance of the corridor so I could inspect their hair for lice. I got my mother's dressmakers' scissors from my locker and the nit comb.

I started with the boys. Their hair was nearly shoulder

length by now. I snipped away and became more adept at what I was doing as the hours went by. After I had shortened their hair considerably, I pulled the nit comb through it. The boys were reasonably clean. Not many had lice in their hair, but when I started on the girls later in the afternoon it was a different story. I was getting very tired, so when the little girls were done I called it a day.

The next morning I continued with the older girls. First I did Phoebe. I cut her hair and then inspected her head for lice. Phoebe shared my bed and I was pleased to find only a few. I removed these with the nit comb and then killed them by squashing them between my finger and thumb nails. I delighted in the sound of the 'click' telling me they were dead. Little did I know that by doing all this I would endanger my life!

That morning I shortened the hair of most of the girls, until I came to Bella. Bella had thick shoulder-length black hair and before I even touched it, I could see the nits stuck on the outside layer. I asked Bella if her head felt itchy.

'Yes,' she said, 'but what can I do?'

'To start with, you can wash it under the tap outside,' I told her.

'Brrr,' Bella said. 'Too cold.'

I had to agree with her. I told her to sit still and I pulled the nit comb through her hair. The result was terrible. The entire comb was covered in lice. I gave up any attempt to kill them and just shook them off the comb onto the floor. Once the lice hit the floor they scattered in all directions, so we tried to stamp on them with our shoes. It was too much. I told Bella that I could not do it. Bella, who was a very easy-going girl, shrugged her shoulders, to show she was not offended.

I went in search of Sister Hermina. I found her in the dining room talking to Sister Hella, who was slowly recovering from the beating she had received from Rau. She managed a wan smile for me. I told Sister Hermina about the condition of Bella's hair and the lice that infested most of us, and I urged her to do something about it. Sister Hermina said she would tell Sister Luba to see what could be done. Two days later four large containers with a gooey yellow ointment arrived, and we were told to smother our hair with it every night.

It was a revolting remedy but it had to be done. Everybody smeared their head with the gooey stuff that night except for those who were sick. Jacky had been one of the first to contract typhus, and over the past few days a few more children had taken to their beds. We also smeared some of the ointment over the joints in the bed frames in an attempt to kill the bedbugs, which gave us no peace at night. The boys grimaced as the gooey mass penetrated their hair. The girls looked disgusted, piling their hair on top of their heads. The older children helped the little ones until we all looked like yellow circus clowns. That night we were in bed later than usual.

Chapter 13

One night in late March, just as the lights were about to be turned out, Sister Mala climbed onto a stool so that she stood above the dormitory beds. She requested silence. When it became quiet she told us that the British army was only about one hundred kilometres away from Belsen. We could not believe it. Someone asked her how she knew this. She told us that there was a clandestine radio in the men's camp and that this was how they had received the information. Could it be true? Could we possibly be free soon? We all talked at once, but Sister Mala warned us to be quiet because the SS were getting very jumpy.

During the past few weeks we'd had many air-raid warnings as English reconnaissance planes had flown over the camp. The SS had given strict instructions not to show any lights during the night, and we were warned that they would shoot anyone who did not comply. We blacked out our windows with blankets every night so that Sister Helen could burn a candle. She needed the light as quite a few children were now seriously ill with typhus.

The SS started to patrol the camp at night. The air reconnaissance increased as the front line came nearer. At times we could hear the thunder of artillery; it was music to our ears. Every night Sister Mala reported to us how close the freedom forces were.

'Children,' she would say, 'seventy kilometres' — and the next night, 'Sixty kilometres.'

For us, it could not be soon enough. The condition of the camp deteriorated by the day. Food was so scarce. People died where they stood. No one cleared the bodies away.

It was 30 March 1945. Sister Luba was exhausted and Sister Hermina took over the task of going to beg for food. She asked me to go with her, and we set off on the long road towards the kitchen. Snow had fallen during the night and the entire camp was covered under a thick blanket of new snow. Our footsteps made no sound. The sky was lead-grey. The air was crisp and it was very still. After about an hour we arrived at the kitchen where Sister Hermina had a long conversation with a Polish man. I couldn't follow what they talked about, but when we left Sister Hermina told me that she could return later in the afternoon to pick up some containers of food for the Children's House. This was good news.

We were walking through a lovely wooded area as we neared the gate of the women's camp when I noticed some dark spots in the snow. On closer scrutiny I realised they were beautiful big potatoes. I darted towards them with a cry of joy and started to pick them up from the ground. One, two, three I had in my hands already. While I was bending down to pick up some more, a dark shadow fell over the pristine snow and a shiny pair of black boots came into my line of vision.

When I slowly straightened up with the potatoes still in my hands, I was standing face to face with the notorious guard Irma Grese. My blood turned to ice and my heart began pounding.

'Well?' she said, demanding an explanation.

Before I could answer her Sister Hermina said, 'Please, the little girl was not stealing. She thought it was a shame to leave good food lying in the snow and she picked it up for the children.'

For a moment Grese looked into my eyes as if to ascertain whether Sister Hermina was telling the truth, then to my complete surprise she said, 'All right, you can pick a few more.'

I could not believe what I heard and made no move to pick up more potatoes.

'You are allowed to pick up some more potatoes,' Sister Hermina said.

I did not trust Grese and, expecting to get a hiding, I bent down and picked up two more potatoes. Sister Hermina prompted me to thank her. I looked up to the woman who had my fate in her hands and said, 'Thank you very much, Frau Hauptaufseherin.'

She nodded, indicating that we were allowed to leave.

I had picked up six potatoes in total and dropped them into my pockets. They were very heavy and I could only walk slowly. My legs started to ache from my ankles to my calves. I told Sister Hermina and she took four of the potatoes from me and put them in her coat pocket. With less weight to carry, I tried to walk faster but could not. My feet were dragging and I developed a terrible headache. I couldn't understand what was wrong with me. Sister Hermina was walking in front of me, urging me to hurry, but I couldn't.

At long last we arrived at the barrack. I went straight to my bed and somehow managed to climb up. I still had some aspirins left, and I took one. With unsteady hands I took off my jumper and slacks and found a flannel pyjama top of my mother's in my locker which I put on. It was much too large for me, but who cared? By now I was shaking uncontrollably, and I realised I had a high fever. I crawled under the blanket. After a while it seemed to be a little easier. I noticed that Max had also taken to his bed.

The news of my illness had spread quickly, and a steady stream of children came to my bed to ask how I was feeling. This was a blessing as they were able to bring me cups of water when I craved them. Max was complaining about his headache and I struggled to the foot end of my bed so I could get to my locker. I took out an aspirin for

Max and handed it across to him. Someone got him some water and after a while I could see him dozing off in an uneasy sleep. Jacky was much better and sitting up in bed.

The fever took hold of me again. My whole body ached and my legs felt like lead. Just before the light went out that night Sister Luba came to my bed and laid a cool hand on my burning forehead. She looked very worried and put a wet facecloth on my forehead to cool it down.

Phoebe woke up early and brought me some water. It was very cold so I managed only a few sips. The rest of the water was used to wet the face washer to cool my head. Someone brought me an extra pillow to raise my head. The headaches were awful and I dared not move a muscle. I had learned before I became sick that the first four days were the worst. If you survived, the fever would break on the tenth day, after which red spots would cover your arms, legs and stomach. I lay on my back with my arms resting against my thighs. My legs were aching so much I could not move them. Now and then I opened my eyes a little. My vision was so blurred that I quickly closed them again.

The day passed slowly although I had no idea of the time. It must have been night as Phoebe had come back to bed. Her climbing onto the bed had awakened me, and when she crawled under the blanket she moved so abruptly that my body could not cope. I asked her to lie still. Phoebe tried not to move, but a healthy body turns regularly while sleeping. So when she turned again, sick as I was, I lost my temper, raised my voice and told her to lie still. Leni, whose bed was directly behind mine, called out and told Phoebe to come and sleep in her bed so I could rest properly. Phoebe groped in the dark and slowly crawled past me into Leni's bed. What a relief it was to lie undisturbed! I dozed off and lost all track of time.

The headache was so bad at times that it seemed as if I was in a black well. It became so quiet in my head that I heard nothing at all. I only knew that I was still alive. When I came back from the darkness I could hear snatches of conversation. One conversation I clearly understood was when Sister Helen said, 'They have closed down the water again, the hellish bastards.'

During the long hours when the fever took hold of my body and mind, someone had given me sips of water and freshened the face washer with cold water, but after a few minutes the face washer became hot so I pulled it off. I had no idea how many days I had been sick when the voice of Sister Luba told me to wake up. Slowly my head cleared a bit and with an effort I opened my eyes. Sister Luba insisted. 'Hetty, wake up. The doctor has come to see you,' she said.

I opened my eyes for a second or two and vaguely saw Sister Luba and Doctor Bimko standing near my bed. I closed my eyes again, drifting away.

'Open your mouth, Hetty. I am going to give you some

grape sugar that the doctor has brought for us,' Sister Luba said.

I opened my mouth and felt a spoonful of a very fine, cold substance.

'Swallow it,' Sister Luba coaxed.

I made an effort to get the substance down my parched throat.

'Here, have a sip of water,' she said, supporting my head as she held the cup to my mouth.

The cold water helped me to swallow, but I was relieved when she lowered my head onto the pillow again. With my eyes closed I could hear her and the doctor go to Max, and all the other children in the dormitory who were sick. The next night and the following night all the sick children received another spoonful of grape sugar in an attempt to give us some energy to fight this dreadful disease.

I had no idea how many days had gone by but one morning I woke up and realised that the fever had left my body. I slowly raised my arms and noticed the telltale red spots of typhus on them. I looked across at Max and asked how he was going.

'I've still got a headache,' he said, 'but it's much better than before.'

I turned onto my side facing the window and fell into a deep, healing sleep.

When I finally awoke, I became aware of what had

taken place around me. I looked out of the window and saw a group of prisoners pushing a cart piled with dead bodies in the direction of the crematorium. It looked icy-cold outside. The SS guard had a white band around his left arm. He was rugged up for the cold and had lifted the collar of his coat to protect his ears. But the poor prisoners! How frightful they looked. Skin over bone, they wore only cotton prison pyjamas and they had to do this gruesome job. The pace was slow but, to my surprise, the Scharführer did not urge the men to hurry. They were too frail to push the cart any faster anyway, and they had to keep stopping every few metres to catch their breath. It was a truly macabre sight.

Sister Hella stood next to my bed. Her whole face was smiling. 'How are you, my Hettylein?' she asked. 'I am so glad you are out of danger, and Max too.'

She walked over to Max and shook up his pillows so he would be comfortable.

Sister Hella told me that all the SS guards had the white bands around their arms as the English army was very close and the guards would surrender. Everybody was waiting apprehensively for what would happen in the next few days. Sister Hella told me that a few days ago male prisoners had dug a huge hole in front of das Revier and that is where the cartload of bodies was being taken — to a mass grave.

I looked outside. A slushy snow was falling and daylight was fading fast.

Someone brought me a small, flat piece of hard-baked flour. It looked like a biscuit but besides being rock-hard, the taste was indescribable as the flour was only half-cooked. It had been cooked and dried on top of the stove in the dining room. There was nothing else to eat. I was told that this had been the only food available for four days and that water was hard to get as well. It had been turned off for two days. Still, the ghastly conditions could not dampen the pervasive feeling of expectation.

We could hear hurried footsteps in the corridor. Silence fell in our dormitory. The footsteps went past our door towards the dining room. We started to speak again as no danger seemed imminent, but then our door opened and Sister Hermina entered with a messenger from Frau Stana. It became quiet again and Sister Hermina told us that our camp would be inspected by the English army the next day. The order from the Commandant was that no one was allowed outside the barracks tomorrow. We were to observe absolute silence during the inspection. Anyone disobeying this order would be shot.

Sister Hermina repeated the order so that we all understood the seriousness of it. It was time to go to sleep. Many of the children were still very sick, though some of us were on the way to recovery. We did not talk much that night; we were all busy with our own thoughts. I asked myself if it really was true that freedom was so close. I was very tired and wanted to go to sleep. As I turned my face towards the window I saw the prisoners were still moving a cart with dead bodies by the light of a kerosene lamp.

The next morning those who were well enough were up early, but we still had some hours to wait before the kapo posted outside our barrack screamed the order to be mouse-still. Everybody in the dormitory froze. Not a sound was heard. For a few minutes the silence continued, but then we heard heavy footsteps approaching. I held my breath, looked out of the window and there they were.

Two SS guards with drawn bayonets marched quickly on either side of a young English soldier carrying a small white flag, his head held proudly high. The SS guards looked very grim. The English soldier stared ahead but now and then his eyes darted over the mountain of dead bodies. The small group passed our barrack very quickly and as I saw them disappear into the distance I wanted to call the English soldier back to give me reassurance that freedom was just around the corner.

As soon as the inspection was over, everybody in the dormitory started to talk at once. Iesy made an effort to walk over to my bed. He was still very weak and had found a stick to support himself. He lifted his head towards me. His deeply sunken eyes with dark lines around emitted a burning light of happiness and hope.

'Hetty, get well soon, it will not be long now and we

shall be free again.' He laughed as only Iesy could laugh when he was sure of something.

I could only nod my head.

Max had not been able to see the inspection party from his bed.

'What did he look like?' he asked, meaning the English soldier.

'He looked good to me,' Iesy said.

'I liked his nose, which he so proudly stuck in the air,' I added.

Everybody laughed.

Sister Luba entered the dormitory and requested our attention. When we quietened down, she told us that no one was allowed to leave the compound. When Sister Luba's mouth was set in a straight line, she was demanding unquestioning obedience. The happy mood disappeared as we realised we were still vulnerable.

Before she left, Sister Luba came to my bed to see how I was recovering. She also looked at Max and Robby and the children in the far corner who were still very ill.

Quiet returned to the dormitory when the children who were not sick left to play outside. You could hear their excited voices, just like normal children at play. Max and Robby had dozed off again, and Iesy had climbed up to his bed to have some rest. I was wide awake but lay very still. The happenings of the morning seemed to have drained the little strength I had. I looked out of the window and saw the mountain of dead bodies. Today there were no prisoners clearing them.

It was as if time stood still. Nothing moved outside. There were only the grey skies and dead bodies. I closed my eyes and in my mind I could see the English soldier with the fierce-looking SS guards. The brief glimpse of them as they marched past my window would be etched into my memory for the rest of my life.

During the day someone brought me some dry flour cookies, but I refused them. I didn't have the strength to chew. So I ate nothing. I was past the stage of feeling hunger. I just wanted to lie in bed and rest. I did not realise how thin I had become and how weak I really was. As usual, some of the children came to my bed now and then to see how I was and to get anything I wanted, such as a cup of water or the potty. They helped me and held me up if I needed the potty. Not even an experienced nurse could have given me better help than the willing hands of the nine- and ten-year-old girls.

Night set in, bringing sleep, and with sleep came forgetfulness and healing for the sick.

On 14 April 1945 the camp grapevine informed us that the SS guards had been replaced with Hungarian soldiers in the watchtowers. The camp itself was very quiet. It was as if everything was in a haze, unreal, waiting for things to happen. I was sleeping a few hours at times, nature's way of making me better.

The night was not peaceful. I could hear machine-guns firing in the distance and wild screams. Sister Mala doused the candle she usually kept burning. She didn't want to attract attention to us during the shooting. I tried to look through the window but it was pitch-black outside. I was so scared that I pulled the blanket over my head as if to ward off evil.

I must have slept, as I woke to the noise of some of the other children. What a relief — daylight. Max was up and about, talking to Leni. When he saw that I was awake, he stumbled over to me, holding onto the bunks for support. I told him to sit on Robby's bed so he could get the weight off his feet for a while. Max sat at Robby's feet and looked up at me.

'How are you today?' he asked.

'I'm not strong enough to get up yet,' I answered.

'Maybe you will be tomorrow,' Max said optimistically.

Iesy also came over. 'Did you hear?' he asked.

'What?'

'That gun firing during the night. It was those Hungarian guards. They shot dead four hundred people. They wanted to go over the fence.'

'How horrible. Is that what all the screaming was about?' I asked.

'Yes,' he said.

We were stunned at the news.

‘Why did the prisoners do it when the English are so close?’ I queried.

‘Yes, why?’ Iesy said. ‘They must have lost their minds at the last moment.’

Max got up and asked Iesy to walk with him to the dining room to see what was happening there. Robby told me he wanted to get up as well, so I called Judy and Phoebe who were nearby and told them to dress Robby warmly. How thin he looked when he emerged from under the blanket. His clothing was too big for him but I was happy to see him on his feet again. Judy took Robby for a walk.

When they left, little Yiddele came shyly towards me. This little three-year-old boy had arrived in our barrack with a Polish and Romanian group of children a few weeks before. They were well-fed and healthy. I could not converse with Yiddele as I could not speak his language, but before I became ill he had attached himself to me.

‘Hello Yiddele,’ I said. ‘It’s good to see you. How are you darling?’

Yiddele looked up at me with big eyes. I had no idea whether he understood me. He was either happy to be close to me again or he was lonely. He never moved from my bed. After a while I told Phoebe to bring a Polish girl to speak to him. The Polish girl came and with sign language I asked her to speak to Yiddele. She bent down and spoke Polish to him, but he looked at her the same way he looked at me and did not speak. After a while the

Polish girl gave up. She looked at me and shrugged her shoulders as if to say, 'I cannot help' and left.

The camp grapevine informed us that the previous night at midnight most of the SS had left the camp. Frau Stania, the camp elder, and many prominents and kapos had gone with them.

It was my mother's birthday, 15 April 1945, and my thoughts lingered on her. Where was she now? I prayed that she would be all right.

The dormitory was very crowded. A lot of children had recovered or were on the way to recovering from typhus, but most of them were not strong enough to venture outside. They chatted among themselves and a feeling of happy expectation prevailed.

It was way past lunchtime but there was nothing to eat. We had had nothing for breakfast either but no one thought about food. An electric feeling was in the air.

It was half past three. I was lying back on my pillow. The excitement had tired me out completely.

'Hetty, Hetty,' I heard.

I lifted my head and I could see Inge trying to get past a group of children. Inge was the Dutchwoman of German origin who, with her friend Gretel, had written Sister Luba's birthday poem for me.

'Oh Inge. How good it is to see you again. Where have you been all this time?' I said.

'I have been very sick but I wanted to see you so much I had to come.'

I looked at Inge. She still looked sick and she was very thin.

'Come Inge,' I said, 'sit on my bed. Here, use the stool.'

Inge climbed onto the stool with difficulty and between us we managed to get her onto my bed. After we both got our breath back, Inge asked, 'Are you all right, Hetty? You still look very sick.'

'I'm fine,' I said. 'Just a bit weak still.'

Before Inge could say anything else, there was a loud disturbance in the corridor. A woman was screaming hysterically in Polish. Silence fell in the dormitory. Then the door flew open and someone shouted, 'The English are here, the English are here!'

For a moment, no one moved, but then everybody who could walk left the barracks and ran as fast as they could towards the fence to see our liberators.

I was sitting on my bed unable to move. My heart was pounding. I would have given anything to be with them, running towards the fence. I looked out of the window and saw that our group had disappeared out of sight already. Only Iesy was still visible, struggling on, leaning on his stick and behind him, as quickly as his little legs could carry him, came Yiddele.

The sight of Iesy struggling through a field of dead bodies and little Yiddele following him brought tears to my eyes, and as I turned towards Inge the realisation that we were free hit me.

'We are free, Inge. We are free,' I cried out.

We were both crying as we embraced each other, rocking to and fro. Freedom! Freedom! At long, long last we were free again.

After a few hours most of the children had returned to our dormitory and told us of the events that had taken place when our liberators had entered the camp. They told us that tanks had come up the main road and an announcement was made over a loudspeaker telling us that we were free. They also told us that English soldiers had immediately taken control over the kitchens, as there was a rumour going around that the SS was cooking poisoned food for us. The kettles had to be cleaned out first and tomorrow there would be food. How they found out all this information no one asked. We really did not care. We were free and the future looked good again.

It was getting dark when Max entered the dormitory. He proudly showed me two pairs of woollen socks and a jumper.

'How did you get them?' I asked.

'The prisoners raided the storeroom,' he said. 'I went in and helped myself.'

I looked at him and realised that he had gone to the far end of the camp. Where in the world did he get this strength from? He had only got up that morning and walked with the aid of a stick, and yet he had run to the fence and, by the sound of it, he had walked a great distance. He was much stronger than I was. I couldn't even attempt to get out of bed, let alone walk.

That night there were no restrictions on bedtime and the Sisters left us to our own devices. Nobody thought of food. Adrenalin kept us going. But in the end, exhaustion took hold. The little ones were put to bed by the older children as I gave out orders from the top of my bed. At long last sleep set in and peace reigned.

Early the next morning there was an exodus from our barrack. All the boys left to find food and to make contact with our liberators again. The little ones stayed behind and played in the compound. During the morning Sister Luba and Sister Hermina came in to see how we were recovering. They did not stay for long as they wanted to go to the kitchen to find something for us to eat. We'd had nothing to eat for two days. Tea had arrived early in the morning and the beaker of hot, sweet liquid had tasted, as my Uncle Max used to say, 'as if an angel landed on your tongue'. You could feel the healing effect as the warmth descended into your empty stomach. I was content to lie in my bed in the now quiet dormitory.

It must have been about midday when I had my first visit from one of our liberators. Surrounded by some of

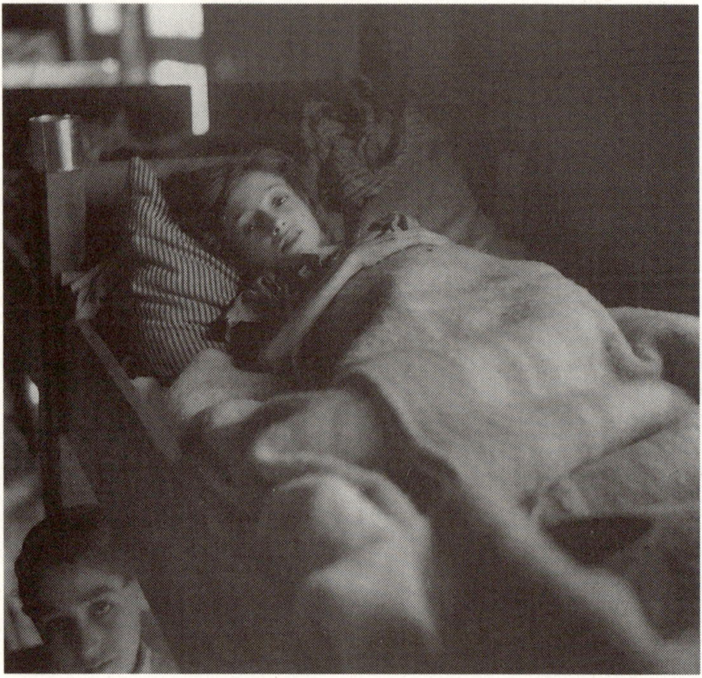

Leni, the day after liberation. Her arm shows the state of emaciation of her body. Jacky is sitting on the lower bunk.

(Courtesy of the British Imperial War Archives)

the children he came to my bed and introduced himself as the Reverend Ted Aplin, a priest from Canada. Communication was difficult as I did not speak English. He asked me if I was okay.

I could understand 'okay' and nodded. The priest then asked me something about Leni. I could not answer him; the reason why I knew he was talking about Leni was because he was pointing at her.

'That's Leni,' I told him.

He studied Leni and I could see the pity in his eyes. Leni looked so frail. She was only skin and bones. A photographer came in and the priest told him to take a picture of Leni. Jacky, who was sitting on the lower bunk, craned his neck so he would be in the picture as well. After taking some more pictures the priest and the photographer left.

About an hour later, a very excited Max came in, and with him was a tall English soldier wearing a purple beret. They came straight to my bed and Max said, 'Hetty, this is Max Monash. He's Dad's cousin.'

'Really?' I asked the smiling soldier, who had a black moustache and warm brown eyes.

'Yes,' he said, 'I believe so. Your father is Maurice, is he not?'

I nodded. My eyes scanned his face, failing to find a family resemblance. Max Monash asked me many questions about my father and whether I knew the whereabouts of different family members. I could only tell him that I did not know what had happened to them. After about half an hour Max Monash left with Iesy and Max. He promised to come back the next day. Before he left he gave me a large block of chocolate, which I shared with some of the children.

When the dormitory became quiet again, I realised that what had impressed me most was the healthy outdoor look Max Monash had. He looked so clean.

I wished I was strong enough to get up. There seemed to be all sorts of things happening outside the barrack.

As promised, Max Monash returned the next day. With him came a few people from the Red Cross. Among them were a young Dutchman called Jaap Ebeling Koning and a Dutch nurse. All the others were English. Jaap's charismatic appeal resulted in a group of children gathering around him. They touched him to make sure he was real, and asked him a thousand questions at once. Jaap was wonderful with the children and gave them all a block of chocolate with the usual warning not to eat it all at once.

After a while Jaap told the healthy children to go and play outside as the sick children in the dormitory needed quiet and rest. Jaap then came over to my bed to ask how I was getting on.

What a kind and wonderful person Jaap was. He was about twenty-one and had joined the Red Cross when the south of Holland was liberated. He had a lovely smile that instantly told you that he could be trusted. Jaap stayed on longer than the others. The living conditions in our barrack had not improved and the smell of sickness and unwashed bodies must have been nauseating, but he didn't care and his happy smile lifted our spirits.

Tuesday, 17 April 1945 started with more tumult. It was a beautiful day. The windows of the dormitory were wide open so the warm, fresh air could enter. In the early hours of the morning trucks laden with dead bodies drove past our barrack. Some SS men could be seen sitting on top of the bodies. The truck was heading towards the mass grave near the crematorium. While this was happening a huge bulldozer arrived and started to dig a second mass grave just in front of my window. A group of about forty Hungarian soldiers marched up to the front of our barrack and were told to line up in two rows. An English officer conducted what appeared to be a rollcall, as one by one Hungarian soldiers would step forward and call out. I had no idea what it meant, but this went on for about an hour until they were marched away towards the morgue.

When the hole was large enough, a truck arrived with decomposed bodies. Six SS men were sitting among the corpses. They were told to unload the truck and put the bodies into the mass grave. The English guards were tense and furious after seeing the atrocities that had been

The SS removing the dead,
with the liberated prisoners looking on.
(Courtesy of the British Imperial War Archives)

committed by the Germans. If an SS man did not move fast enough or dropped an arm onto the ground while carrying a corpse, they would lash out at them with the butt of their rifles. The SS showed signs of being under pressure. Their previously spotless uniforms were dirty and in disarray.

One SS man still had his cap on, which made an English soldier posted just in front of my window so furious that, with a swipe of his rifle, narrowly missing the man's head, he removed the cap. It spiralled into the air, landing on my windowsill. On seeing the result of his action, the English soldier ran towards my window and, after saluting me, removed the cap with the end of his rifle.

Throughout the day, the SS brought the bodies to the mass grave. These SS officers, who had always stayed at a safe distance from the macabre mess so they would not contaminate themselves, were now standing knee-deep among the decaying corpses.

I only witnessed the burial, but was later told that at the morgue where the bodies were loaded onto the trucks, the English soldiers occasionally gave the SS a good hiding for not handling the corpses with more respect.

The next morning the burying of the dead continued, but the English did not hit the SS any more, by order of their superiors and the Geneva Convention. What a shame. The prisoners had enjoyed it.

I was still confined to my bed. The burial of thousands of

The mass grave in front of the Children's House.
Hetty's bed was behind the open window, second from the left.
(Courtesy of the British Imperial War Archives)

bodies just outside the windows of our barrack continued. I turned my back to the window: seeing body after body being dumped one on top of the other in the huge grave was upsetting. Since our liberators were being restrained from harassing the SS, they were not as careful now. It all became too much. I was still very weak from the devastating illness. I could not remember if I'd had anything to eat that day or, for that matter, the past few days. Everything was shrouded in a haze. So many things had happened. But, come what may I decided, tomorrow I would get up.

The following day I waited until the dormitory was nearly empty and then prepared to leave my bed. From the locker I took out my grey chequered skirt and my jumper, and dressed myself on top of my bed, the same way as I had for the past seventeen months. When I was ready I carefully lowered myself from my bed onto the chair next to it. From there I could easily reach the floor while still holding onto my bunk for support. As I stood shakily on the floor, my skirt dropped around my ankles, and it was then that I realised that I had lost a lot of weight. My skirt was far too big for me. My coat was hanging on the end of my bed and I remembered that under the collar was a safety pin I used to pin up my collar when the bitter wind was blowing during rollcall. I transferred the safety pin from my coat to hold up my skirt. So far, so good.

I attempted to walk but my legs felt so rubbery I could

One of the children of the Children's House,
Siegfried Maandag, seven years old, walks past the corpses
of Bergen-Belsen after the Liberation.
20 April 1945.

(Photograph by George Rodger; Time/Life; Getty Images)

hardly stand. I moved my feet slowly, holding onto the bunks on either side of the walkway.

'Good, Hetty, I'm glad to see you up again,' Leni said, who had been watching my progress from her bed.

I smiled up at her as I slowly shuffled past. By now I had reached the door, and when I entered the corridor there was no one in sight. I turned towards the dining room, holding onto the wall for support. When I reached the end of the corridor, I peeped into the dining room, but it was deserted. Everybody was out. I decided to go into the toilet, which was partitioned off at the end of the corridor by a crude wooden door. There was no such thing as a water-closet, only a bucket with a wooden plank over it. Nevertheless, it meant privacy. I sat down on the plank, and it was from this place that I prayed and thanked God for our freedom and asked him to look after my father and my mother, to keep them safe and bring them home again.

My emotions overtook me and hot tears fell down my cheeks. After a while I calmed down and dried my tears with the sleeve of my jumper. I sat for a few more minutes and when I left the toilet I closed the door firmly behind me.

Slowly I walked back along the dark corridor towards the open door and daylight. I wanted to get into the fresh air. As I neared the doorway an English soldier entered. For a moment he stood still, letting his eyes become accustomed to the darkness. He came towards me and asked in German, 'Are you Hetty?'

‘Yes,’ I answered.

‘Good,’ the soldier said. ‘I want you to come with me. The children have sent me. We asked them to sing for us but they won’t do it without you.’

For a moment I hesitated. I still felt suspicious and fearful. ‘Where are the children?’ I asked.

Sensing my unease, the soldier smiled at me and said, ‘Don’t be scared. I’ll take you to them. They are just a bit further up the road.’

He stuck out his hand to help me down the few steps into the compound, and I walked very slowly towards the gate. Seeing that I could not walk very well the soldier did not waste any more words. He lifted me in his arms and carried me down the road to where the children had gathered around an army jeep. Carefully, he sat me down on the end of the jeep.

The children crowded around, and Max told me that the soldiers wanted us to sing for the radio but they had not been able to decide what to sing. After some deliberation, ‘Ferdinand Was a Bull’ was chosen. This was a song from the Dutch singing duo Johnny & Jones, who were sent to Auschwitz. And, of course, we would also sing ‘Barrack Seventeen’.

After a few false starts, the song was recorded. When the soldiers were satisfied with the recording, one of them asked me some questions in German and then suggested we record it. I told him that my German was very limited, but he said that was okay.

The soldier who had carried me over was still there and he smiled encouragingly at me. The recorder was ready and the soldier asked the first question:

'What is your name?'

'Hetty Werkendam,' I answered.

'How old are you?' he asked.

'I am fifteen years old.'

The interview continued; we did it twice to make sure it came out all right. The soldiers thanked me and the one who had carried me earlier took me back to the barrack.

Little did I realise that this interview would be broadcast all over the world. I was later told that family and friends from as far away as Argentina, Belgium, Holland and Sweden heard me speak on the radio, and this way the few family members who had been spared found out that I was still alive.

Chapter 14

It was Saturday, 21 April 1945, my father's birthday. The sun was shining brightly when early in the morning ambulances and trucks arrived to take us away to another place. Soldiers with Red Cross bands on their arms came into the dormitory and told us to leave everything behind. We must come in the clothes we were wearing. They told us this was to prevent the typhus from spreading.

The trauma from earlier evacuations were still fresh in our minds. Those who could walk and were okay went onto the trucks first, including Max and Jacky. I called out from the window for them to take me as well, but the truck moved on without me. I came down from my bed as quickly as I could, but I was still too weak to walk very far. When I stopped to catch my breath, a soldier lifted me in his arms and took me to the waiting ambulance. I looked around and saw that Leni and Maurice were already inside. Both were lying on stretchers, and about ten other children were sitting on the floor.

Suddenly I realised that I had left Robby inside. I made

an attempt to leave the ambulance but was prevented from doing so by a Red Cross soldier. I begged him to find Robby for me. I was quite hysterical by now and kept calling for Robby at the top of my voice. Seeing my distress, the soldier told someone to go inside to find Robby for me. He also told the driver, who was anxious to drive off with his load of sick children, to wait.

After about five minutes the soldier who had gone in search of Robby returned with him and Yiddele as well. How happy I was to see the two little ones. They were lifted into the ambulance and both snuggled up to me. How in the world could I forget about them, I scolded myself.

The ambulance started and we left this place of horrors. The ambulance had no back doors so we could see where we were going. Soon we left concentration camp Bergen-Belsen behind and were driving on a bitumen road. After a very short drive we entered what we were later told was a German officers' barracks, with well-kept red-brick two-storey buildings with gardens and lawns. The ambulance stopped and soldiers and nurses helped us out and took us into a building which had sunlight streaming through its high windows. I was lifted onto a table where a doctor examined me. My weight was recorded as thirty-four kilograms. I was then told to stand still and a soldier came forward with what appeared to be a vacuum cleaner. The nurse held the hose under my skirt while the soldier puffed a cloud of grey powder. The process was repeated on the front and back of my jumper, and my hair got a dosing of this strange-smelling powder as well. It was only much later that I learned the powder was DDT. I stood there in the grey haze until the nurse guided me outside where I was glad to breathe clean air again.

Outside were long tables with lots and lots of clothing in every size and colour, and everybody could pick out clean things to wear.

It was then that I realised that I had forgotten to take my mementoes from my locker: Herman's Swann pen and his watch with his photograph on the dial face. I had left them behind in the panic to get into the ambulance to follow Max and Jacky. I was so upset that I started to cry. Tears were never far away then. Sister Luba asked what was the matter. Through my tears I told her.

'Come,' Sister Luba said, 'our new house is about a hundred metres from here.'

She took me by the hand and slowly we walked across a grass field towards a two-storey building. Sister Luba promised that she would send someone down to the camp to find the pen and the watch. I knew well enough that once we left the Children's House the ex-prisoners would swoop like vultures to see if there was anything that could be of use to them.

We entered our new home and I was so happy to see Sister Hermina, so clean and dressed in a white nurse's apron. Her thick wavy hair was pulled back from her face and she looked really pretty. She smiled when she saw me come in with Sister Luba. I told her about my distress at losing my precious mementoes of my friend Herman. She put her arm around me, and Sister Luba told her that she would send someone back to see if they could be found.

Sister Hermina took me to the kitchen, the first room next to the entrance. Inside the kitchen was a long table with chairs around it. She told me to sit down, and after a few seconds put a bowl of porridge in front of me and a beaker of hot tea. I could only eat about two spoonfuls.

When I was finished Sister Hermina took me up a flight of stairs. I had to pull myself up holding onto the bannister. I entered a lovely room, which had only two beds with snow-white sheets. I could not believe my eyes.

'Am I to sleep here?' I asked Sister Hermina.

'Yes,' she said. 'One of the Hungarian girls will share the room with you.'

I went over to the bed and stroked the white sheets. They smelt so nice. Sister Hermina said that we must go down again to see if the other children had arrived.

My God, I thought, where are Max and Jacky?

I had also forgotten about Robby and Yiddele again. I followed Sister Hermina downstairs, holding onto the bannister with both hands. The hall was crowded as most of the children had arrived. Sister Luba was standing in the middle. There were also some English nurses who helped to find everybody a place to sleep in one of the many rooms of the building. I saw Iesy and asked him if he had seen my brothers.

'Yes,' he said. 'They went to explore the camp. They're okay. They'll come back,' he assured me. 'Don't worry.'

It was strange to sleep in a separate room instead of a dormitory. I also felt far removed from Max and Jacky. But the cool sheets and clean pyjamas felt so good that I soon fell asleep and did not wake up until late next morning

The weather was drizzly and the sky was grey. Most of the children were playing and running around on the soaking grass in front of the house. I dozed off again and must have gone into a deep sleep because when I woke, it was late afternoon.

The Hungarian girl came back when darkness fell. She was a big girl and already very sophisticated. She had arrived in Belsen about four weeks before the liberation. She had not lived through the long months of deprivation, hunger and despair. She was robust and energetic. We could converse in German with a very limited vocabulary. When she entered the room she unloaded packet after packet of cigarettes from her pocket and the inside of her blouse onto her bed. I watched in astonishment.

'What are you doing with all those cigarettes?' I asked. 'Do you smoke?'

'No,' she answered, 'but when I get home these cigarettes will be worth a lot of money and I can buy food with them.

I am asking every soldier for cigarettes.'

I had never thought of doing this. Children from Eastern Europe were much more streetwise than those of us who came from Western Europe. When the Hungarian girl stashed the cigarettes in a nearly full pillowslip, I decided that I would also ask for cigarettes to take home with me.

I was sitting on a chair in the hall. My right arm was aching as I had been writing nonstop for three days. Jaap Ebeling Koning had come in one day and asked me if I could write down my experiences in Bergen-Belsen. He explained it was a request from English military headquarters to ensure that the horrors of the camp were properly recorded for the future. How could I refuse a request from our liberators? Jaap brought me pen and paper and installed me in a small room next to the stairs where I was not disturbed. Now and then a nurse would bring me tea or a sandwich. They asked how I was progressing and told me to take it easy.

I was still tiring quickly and wasn't able to eat well. The Red Cross nurses attempted to persuade me to try some porridge or anything else I wanted. One morning I asked them for a fried egg. For many months in the camp I'd had a great desire to eat an egg. The nurse who sat next to me smiled happily when she gave my request to the cook, but when the egg was put in front of me a few minutes later, I could not eat it. The smell of food made me sick and no persuasion could make me taste it.

From where I was sitting in the hall, I could look through the open front door and see the children playing on the field. Max and Jacky and some other boys had left in the morning to go 'exploring', as they called it. Now and then they would return and bring me the latest news of what they had seen and experienced.

The drizzly weather continued but I decided to go outside for some fresh air. I noticed that some English soldiers were erecting swings for the children. How wonderful our liberators were. I watched them for a while but then I could feel the chill in the air penetrating my clothes again so I returned indoors.

I was about halfway down the hall when I heard someone call my name. I turned and saw Leni's brother, Maurice. It dawned on me that I had not seen Maurice around lately.

'Hi, Maurice,' I said. 'Where have you been?'

'I've been in the hospital,' he answered. 'Leni is dead, Hetty, Leni is dead.'

He looked so skinny and his coat was miles too big for him. His shoulders were drooping and the tears were running down his hollow cheeks. My weakness forgotten, I ran to him and put my arms around him, while he unburdened his immense grief. When Maurice lifted his tear-stained face, I asked him, 'When did she die?'

'About two days ago.'

'Do you know where they buried her?' I asked.

Maurice shook his head, unable to speak.

'Don't worry,' I told him. 'We'll find out.'

Maurice nodded again, still unable to speak. I told a nurse who was walking by that Maurice had just come from the hospital and needed a bed.

I honestly do not know what happened to me during this emotional release with Maurice, but afterwards I felt much stronger and capable of doing things for the children again. Maurice needed me, and I had to be strong to be able to find Leni's grave for him. When Maurice returned, we both went to the kitchen where, for the first time, I was able to eat a bowl of porridge without feeling sick.

I went to Sister Luba's room to tell her the sad news about Leni. Her room was next to the kitchen and when I entered there were lots of people inside. As well as Sisters Luba, Hermina and Hella, there were three English officers and a Canadian officer.

The radio was on, tuned to a German station and the broadcaster was announcing that the Russians were approaching Berlin from the east and northern gates. The room fell silent and everybody listened to the news. The announcer was calling all boys over twelve to be mobilised to defend Berlin against the Russians. Suddenly the broadcast was interrupted: an English voice announced that Hitler was dead, immediately followed by the English national anthem. The soldiers left, and we talked about the latest development, but it really did not matter to us what was happening in Berlin. For Belsen the war ended on 15 April 1945.

It was a warm spring and we were standing in the hall when Iesy declared that he wanted some chicken soup. 'So why don't we go and steal a chicken from a farmhouse?' he said.

Everybody agreed but I said, 'First we have to find where Leni is buried.'

Our group that day consisted of Iesy, Max, Jacky, Maurice, Louky and me. We crossed the field and walked through a wooded area towards the outskirts of the camp. How good it felt to be walking about in freedom.

Before long we noticed a small clearing with a white picket fence and we could see it was a graveyard. We entered it and a man crossed the clearing and came towards us. He asked us in Polish what we wanted, or that is what we thought he asked. Believing that he might be the guardian of the cemetery, I handed him a piece of paper with Leni's name on it. He walked away to a small shed under the trees and when he returned he pointed to a place in the second row of freshly dug graves.

We all stood there in silence and reflected on the sad fact that Leni was not able to be with us in freedom.

Maurice stood with bowed head but did not cry. He had no tears left. I could see that he was relieved to know the place where Leni was resting. I turned around and noticed the trees nearby and registered in my mind the distance her grave was from the entrance. I wanted to remember where we had to leave our Leni behind.

After we left the cemetery, Iesy reminded us that we still had to find a chicken. We followed the road and slowly our mood lifted. Fifteen minutes later we came upon a farmhouse. It must have been midday as the farmer and his family were having their lunch on the grass in the warm sun. As we approached the family retreated to the house except for a young girl of about twelve. She remained seated and looked at us curiously. She, like the others of her family, looked chubby and rosy with health. They had not starved during the war. They were well fed. How could one believe that they had not heard or known what had happened in Belsen, only a few miles away?

The father came back to tell the girl to come inside. Iesy approached the father and asked if we could have a chicken. The father shook his head and urged his daughter to hurry. They quickly moved into the house and closed the door firmly behind them. For a while we stood there, undecided about what to do next. Here and there we saw a chicken scurrying beside the house but we still had the terror of 'the regime' inside us, and despite our earlier bravado, we were too scared to take one.

We continued our walk. The road was deserted and the sun-drenched fields stretched out before us. Except for the singing of the birds, no other sound was heard.

'We can't see any other houses and we're tired. I think we had better get back,' Max said.

Maurice and Louky agreed. Without noticing it we had wandered a long way from the recuperation camp. We could not even see it any more in the distance.

I was standing at the rear of our small group when I saw a movement in the high grass. Suddenly two English soldiers approached us with drawn rifles, looking very menacing as they came near. I felt the hair rise on the nape of my neck and realised the danger we were in.

'Stop! Don't move!' one soldier called.

The six of us stood frozen on the spot. While the first soldier kept us covered, the second soldier asked for our papers.

'No papers, children of Children's House, Bergen-Belsen,' I told him.

That seemed to mean something to him, as he turned around and called out to what appeared to be an empty field. Six other soldiers became visible and approached us with their guns at the ready. They formed a circle around us and one soldier who looked as if he was in charge asked roughly, 'Where are you going and who are you?'

I was terrified and started to tremble. Iesy said, 'We are from the Children's House of Bergen-Belsen.'

The soldiers discussed this answer and then one said, 'Go, go, go!' and pointed in the direction of our camp.

We didn't need to be told twice — we ran as fast as our legs would carry us. Unwittingly, we had walked straight into the path of a patrol party. We had forgotten that there was still a war going on, and we must have crossed the demarcation line of the forty square kilometres the Germans had surrendered unconditionally to the English before Belsen was freed.

We were out of breath by the time we were close to our camp again. We were telling each other how lucky we had been when we heard a motorcycle approaching fast. We looked over our shoulders and a soldier on a bike came into view. He shouted, 'Hey, hey!'

We started to run away, but the soldier kept calling, 'Hey, children. Children,' he called, 'the war is over!'

We looked at each other but could not understand what he was trying to tell us. He then raised his arm pretending it was a rifle and called out, 'Bang, bang, bang — finished!' waving his arms in the air.

Max understood it first. 'Hetty!' he screamed, 'the war is finished!'

We jumped up and down from happiness and screamed our throats hoarse, then ran towards our building, yelling out the good news as we passed the soldiers' tents.

'The war is over, the war is over!' we told Sister Luba as we burst into her room. What happiness! We laughed, we kissed, we danced and sang. All the bottled-up emotions came rushing out and we thanked God for saving our lives.

The next day on the field across from our house twenty huge field guns were set up in two rows. There was to be an official ceremony to herald the end of the war.

At six o'clock that night we all lined up to see the show. Jeeps arrived with high-ranking officers to witness the salute to the end of the war. There was no dais or microphone. We could faintly hear a man speaking, after which all the British military present gave three loud cheers. Then a trumpet sounded 'The Last Post' and silence fell for two minutes. A command was given and a soldier waved a white flag. The soldiers who had stood to attention next to the guns, sprang into action. Each cannon fired twenty-one times. The noise was unbearable. We covered our ears, to no avail. The earth was trembling, the air was black and smelled putrid, but then it was over and quiet descended.

Within the hour the field was empty except for the empty brass shells which the cannons had ejected after each shot. Max, Jacky and I each picked up a shell, a souvenir of the end of the war and a symbol of our freedom. I held the now harmless shell and planted a big kiss on it.

Now that the war was over, most of the soldiers were relieved of duty and had more free time. Many of them visited the Children's House and they brought us presents and sweets. They put up a table tennis table on the field and Jacky became quite an expert.

One day a film crew arrived and I was the only one around, sitting on a chair in the hall. They asked me to come outside on the swings, where a nice soldier gently pushed me. After a short while I had to ask him to stop as I was getting dizzy. I was still not completely recovered, although I was eating much better. The children who had been invisible a moment earlier now seemed to appear as if by magic. They all wanted to have a turn on the swings so they could become film stars. I went inside to call Sister Luba; she was the heart of the Children's House and had to be in the film with us. The film crew turned their camera on the table tennis, where Jacky performed like a pro.

The days and weeks went by and slowly we became stronger. Our cheeks filled out and our bodies became fuller. The warm, sunny days helped to restore our health and our minds to a certain extent. At times, one could still hear a child screaming in terror during the night but slowly we emerged from the trauma.

I had asked Jaap a few times when he thought we could go home, but he only smiled and told me to be patient. I adored Jaap and so did all the children. We crowded around him whenever he came and we felt a sense of loss when he had to go again.

Earlier Jaap had told us to write letters to anyone we wished to inform that we were still alive. I had written a letter to the Pomstra family in Amsterdam advising them of our whereabouts, and also telling them our worries about our parents and our doubts that they would still be alive.

The recuperation camp was no longer crowded as ex-prisoners were repatriated to their homelands.

Towards the end of May Jaap came to see us with Captain Samuel Gassan. The Captain was Dutch and had joined the Allied forces during the war. He was surprised and very happy that we had survived the horrors of Belsen, and when he left he promised us he would arrange for our quick return to Holland. Jaap escorted him to his car and returned to us after the captain drove off.

'When do you think we will leave, Jaap?' I asked.

'Soon, I think,' he answered with a smile. 'I'll let you know when I find out.'

He ruffled my hair and I leaned against him. My thoughts were in turmoil now that the day was coming that we would return to Holland, leaving everything we had become accustomed to. I looked up at Jaap and asked, 'Do you think we could take Sister Luba with us?'

'I believe we could take her if she wants to come,' Jaap said.

We looked at each other, then, without saying a word, we both turned and walked to Sister Luba's room. Sister Luba looked up in surprise when we entered followed by Max, Iesy and Louky. Iesy told her that Captain Gassan was arranging for our speedy departure to Holland and that we did not want to leave her behind.

'Sister Luba, you must come with us,' Iesy said.

We all nodded our heads in agreement. Sister Luba was deeply touched by our devotion and without hesitation she said, 'Yes, I will come with you.'

One by one she hugged us, and happiness was shining from our eyes. We were going home and the woman who had become our second mother and saved us from starvation in Belsen was coming with us.

The days were passing fast. Jaap told us at the end of May he might be released so that he could accompany us to Holland. I was so happy when he told me this news as I had dreaded the moment when we would have to say goodbye.

On the last day of May, Jaap came to tell us that we had to be ready to leave on 3 June. This was it. The moment was near when we could leave all the nightmares behind us and return to our country. Excitement ran high.

The last days went by fast. We had no packing to do as the only things we possessed were the clothes we were wearing. We were full of anticipation, and the hours could not go quickly enough for us to leave this place forever. Sister Luba ordered everybody to bed early that night.

I could not sleep. My thoughts kept me awake. We are going home in the morning, I kept telling myself. But where were my father and my mother? Were they still alive? I had made an unsuccessful attempt to find them through the Red Cross. I kept turning from side to side and sleep eluded me. My heart was pounding and I could not relax. The night seemed endless, but at long last I could see the dawn breaking and I slid from my bed. I suddenly thought of Sister Hermina, who had always been so good to me, and Sister Hella and her mother, Zosua, and Helen — they had all become dear to me and today I had to say farewell to them. Tears came to my eyes even thinking about it.

I went downstairs. The house was quiet, but when I neared the kitchen I could see a light. The cook — Cookie —was there before me. She gave me a warm smile when I entered the kitchen. Cookie was from the English military. She was about forty, a sturdy, strong woman. She had been allocated to us from the very first day we arrived, and she made sure that we were eating good, wholesome food.

Cookie put a steaming cup of tea in front of me and asked, 'Fried eggs or boiled?'

I shook my head:, 'It's too early for eggs, just toast and jam, please.'

'You're going home today,' Cookie said. 'Are you happy?'

'Yes, I am so happy that I couldn't sleep last night, but I am also very sad.'

'Why?' Cookie asked, looking surprised.

'Because I have to say goodbye to a lot of people I love

and who care for me. I know that I'll never see them again,' I said.

Cookie came and sat opposite me at the table. 'Hetty,' she said, 'you're going home and I hope you will find your father and your mother again, so forget the past and look to the future. We fought to have a better world. Now you make it so, you hear me?'

I nodded my head.

'Drink your tea,' Cookie ordered. 'I have to attend to the breakfast because in a moment the whole bunch will be in.'

Most of the children were dressed and waiting in the hall. Excitement was at a peak.

Jaap arrived at about eight o'clock and told me he was coming with us. What a surprise! Jaap had become very dear to me since the liberation, as well as a trusted and kind friend of all the children. When the good news spread that Jaap was joining us, the children were elated and crowded around him.

The hall had become very full now. All the Sisters — Hermina, Hella and her mother, Maria, Helen and Zosua — as well as a few English nurses and Cookie had come into the hall to spend the last minutes with us.

Sister Luba and Sister Hermina were standing close together. Tears were in Hermina's eyes as she softly talked to Sister Luba. At her feet was a large army bag, which she had filled with flour, sugar and a few bread loaves. Cookie had made lots of sandwiches for us to eat on the road. Suddenly the trucks were there. One by one the children walked past the Sisters and thanked them for their care. When my turn came, I thanked and kissed Sister Hella and her mother, after which I passed all the Sisters until I came to Sister Hermina. I buried my face in her stomach while I was hugging her around her waist, and I did not want to let her go. I lifted my tear-stained face and Sister Hermina bent down to me and said, 'My darling Hettylein, stay well. I love you.' She kissed me and I hugged her more tightly, then with a great effort I let go and went outside to the trucks.

Sister Luba and I were the last to climb into the second truck. Captain Gassan and Jaap were in charge of the first truck. All the Sisters and nurses had come outside to wave us a final farewell. 'Goodbye, goodbye, *auf wiedersehen*,' we called until the small group was no longer visible. At long last we were on our way.

At two o'clock on 3 June 1945 we arrived at Lüneburg airfield. Some soldiers helped us off the truck. We stood huddled together and watched the planes coming and going. The airfield had a single runway and its only building was a galvanised iron shed. Captain Gassan entered the shed to find out when a plane would be available to take us to Holland. He returned about fifteen minutes later and told us we would be leaving after the next plane arrived.

At about half-past two a few soldiers guided us through the field towards the waiting plane. On its side was painted a large circle in red, white and blue. A door at the rear of the plane was open and small steps led up to it. It was the first time any of us had been on a plane. There were long benches on each side of the plane along the metal body, with wooden ribs showing and small windows.

Soon the door was securely closed and we hustled down the runway. We were seated on the long benches with no seatbelts. This military plane had no luxuries. The engines roared and the plane took to the air. The plane was not soundproof or pressurised. The noise of the engines was deafening and we had to yell at each other to be heard. Soon the plane reached its required height and the shaking we'd felt earlier stopped. We could see the enormous damage the Allied bombers had done to the German cities as we flew over them.

The plane landed in Eindhoven. Willing hands helped us down the steps as we finally set foot on Netherlands soil again.

Chapter 15

We were ushered into a building and towards a long table where a few men and women kept records of our arrival. When it was my turn I sat down on the chair with Max and Jacky standing close beside me. The lady asked me my name, my date of birth, and my last address in Holland before our deportation. She asked the names of my parents and in which camp we had been. She wrote everything down and then she wrote out a white card, gave it to me and told me to see the doctor, pointing towards a man dressed in a white coat. I waited for Max and Jacky to be interviewed and when they received their repatriation cards, we walked over to the doctor together. A nurse told us to take off our tops and one by one we were put in front of an X-ray machine to screen our lungs for tuberculosis or other illnesses.

The process was quick. The doctor called out his findings, which the nurse noted on our repatriation cards. A second doctor checked our throats, ears and hands. The nurse recorded everything. Thank God, Max, Jacky and I were free of TB. A few of our children were not so lucky and they were immediately separated from the healthy children.

When it was Sister Luba's turn to be interviewed, we struck trouble. She was Polish and had no right to enter Holland. This had not even occurred to us in our desire to take her home. She was our second mother and we did not care if she was Polish, Russian or Chinese. She had saved our lives and we wanted to keep her with us.

The children thronged around Sister Luba, insisting she should be allowed to stay. In the end, a tall gentleman wearing a gaberdine raincoat came into the room and the staff asked him for advice. He took one look at the agitated faces of the children and told the staff to allow Sister Luba to come with us. What a relief! Soon we all left the room and boarded a waiting truck. We were driven through Eindhoven to a building that appeared to be a school.

We entered a large room with straw mattresses on the floor covered with grey army blankets. Toilet facilities were outside. The whole place looked desolate and grey. When Sister Luba saw how we were received she became very upset and asked me, 'Why did they take us away from our comfortable house in the recuperation camp? This is a terrible place. Even in Belsen I made sure you had beds to sleep in and now you all have to sleep on the floor.' Sister Luba's mouth was set in a straight line.

The news that children had arrived from Bergen-Belsen

spread like wildfire through Eindhoven and scores of people came to the school to meet the children. They opened their hearts and doors, and took most of the children home with them. The repatriation staff was kept busy recording their whereabouts. Only a few children were left behind in Sister Luba's care — our usual group of Max, Jacky, Iesy Louky, Gerry, Maurice and me — I did not even contemplate leaving Sister Luba.

As night fell we turned to the dismal-looking dormitory and made ourselves comfortable on the straw mattresses. Nobody had bothered to bring us any food and it was only thanks to Cookie's sandwiches that we did not go hungry.

We were up and about at dawn the next morning, only to discover that the Dutch authorities had locked us in for the night. We hung around until someone came to open the door and brought us milk and sandwiches. It was a meagre meal.

At ten o'clock the man in the gaberdine raincoat came to see us again. He told us that he was the head of staff, Dr J van Waldre de Bordes. He asked us a lot of questions about Belsen and told us how happy he was that we were safely back in Holland.

When I asked him when we could go to Amsterdam, he told me that Amsterdam was not open for repatriation. There was a lot of sickness and not enough food available, so we had to be a bit patient.

Jaap came by later in the morning. He told me that he

was leaving to go back home to his family in Arnhem. How sad I was to say goodbye to this friend who had won our hearts and our trust as no other liberator had. I knew that I would never see him again, but I also knew that his memory would always remain in my heart.

Sister Luba was not happy. She was restless and had not taken kindly to the authorities, who left us to cater for ourselves. No proper food had arrived. There were no proper ablution facilities. The sleeping quarters were disgusting. The situation did not shock us as we had experienced worse, but Sister Luba was furious and could not excuse the unhygienic conditions. She was also upset because the reason that she had come with us to Holland was to be near us. This need was taken away when the children were fostered out.

I could hear Sister Luba talking to Iesy and Max in the little front room-cum-kitchen. I could hear Iesy loudly protesting about something with Max joining in. As I entered the room I could see the upset faces of Max and Iesy, and the determined look on Sister Luba's face. I looked questioningly from one to the other and Iesy burst out, 'She wants to go back to Belsen. You talk to her please, Hetty, tell her we don't want her to leave!'

My heart contracted. 'No, Sister Luba,' I said, 'you must not go. You must stay with us.'

But I could see from Sister Luba's face that I could not

change her mind. We were desperate. The loss of Sister Luba would mean the loss of our security. All the people who had played such a vital part in our lives during the past eight months had gone away. All the Sisters in Belsen, Jaap and now Luba. Our whole world collapsed, and all our pleading and tears did not help us. Sister Luba wanted to leave as she did not feel needed.

When Dr van Waldre de Bordes came to see us, we implored him to persuade Sister Luba to stay, but nothing could make her change her mind. By the time the doctor left, he had promised Sister Luba that he would arrange for her return to Belsen.

Two days later she left. The farewells were quick and painful. A kiss and a hug for all of us and she hurried away towards the plane. We stood in stunned silence watching the plane take off with the woman who had become our mother in Belsen. We felt bereft. It was the end of an era and the start of an uncertain future.

Dr van Waldre came to see us every day to inquire how we were doing. Whenever he came we asked him when we could go to Amsterdam. Finally, one morning he told us the long-awaited news: we would leave for Amsterdam in two days' time.

The journey to Amsterdam took hours. All the bridges in Holland had been blown up either by the bombs of the

Allied forces or the retreating German army, and all traffic had to be ferried across the rivers. It meant many hours of delay but at last we drove into Amsterdam. It was about four o'clock when the bus came to a stop at the Jewish hospital. The doors of the hospital were closed and only ten people were there to welcome us home. Six people were there to collect children who were related to them, and the other four people were from the Dutch Resistance, which had done much heroic work during the occupation.

Some of our children recognised their relatives and tearful reunions took place. Robby clung to me and I picked him up, understanding his panic among these strange surroundings and people. An elderly couple came up to me and asked if this was Robby Englander.

'Yes,' I said, 'this is Robby.'

'We are his grandparents,' the woman told me.

My heart stopped as I realised that I had to surrender Robby. Robby clamped his little arms around my neck. He buried his head in my shoulder and cried bitterly. His grandmother looked bewildered and stretched her arms out to Robby, who cried even louder. With Robby in my arms I walked to the edge of the group, talking softly to him. I told him that those people were his grandparents and they loved him as much as I did.

'Don't be scared, darling. Dry your tears and go with them and I'll soon come to see you again.'

Robby calmed down. He trusted me. I kissed him and

whispered, 'I love you, darling, be good.'

After about an hour there was only Iesy, Max, Jacky and me left. The woman in charge was called Miep and she asked Iesy if he had somewhere to go.

'Yes,' Iesy said. 'I have the address of my uncle in Amsterdam South.'

'Good,' Miep said, 'my friend will take you there.'

Our farewell was swift. Iesy kissed me on both cheeks. 'Look after yourself, okay?'

I nodded, realising that our close-knit group had disintegrated on our arrival in Amsterdam. Iesy climbed onto the back of the girl's bike and waved goodbye as he disappeared down the street.

'Hetty, have you got somewhere to go?'

'Yes,' I said, 'We have to go to the Pomstra family. They live on the President Steyn Plantsoen.'

'Okay,' Miep said, 'but I'll take you to my place first.'

We walked to Miep's home. It was nearly seven o'clock by the time we arrived. Wearily we climbed the stairs to the first floor and entered a gloomy-looking apartment.

We sat in the front room overlooking the Amstel, and were given a slice of bread and a cup of water. We were very tired, as it had been a long day. I kept telling Miep that I had to go to the Pomstras. Now that I was so close to them, I could not wait to see them.

Miep told us that there was still a curfew. Nobody was allowed on the street from eight o'clock at night until six o'clock in the morning. However Miep, who had been an active member of the Resistance, had permission to be on the street after the curfew.

So, shortly after the curfew started, Miep and I rode through the deserted streets of Amsterdam. Miep had fastened a small pillow to the back of her bike to soften the bumps in the road. The bike had wooden tyres and the ride was rather hazardous. When we drove through the Sarphatistraat towards the Weesperplein it was not so bad as the road was bitumen. But when we turned into the Wieboutstraat, the ride became very bumpy and painful. I cannot describe in a few words the emotions I felt when we rode over the Wieboutstraat. I had walked home that way from school with my girlfriends many times — girlfriends whose lives had ended violently. Although it was about half-past eight, it was still daylight and I could clearly see the diggings people had made on the land next to the road in search of coal during the winter. The area we drove past had been used for decades as a place for the trains to park and reverse before the new railway line and subways were built just before the war. When we drove past Luyks, the mustard factory, I knew we did not have far to go. Then we were in the subway. At the end of the subway we would ride into the President Steyn Plantsoen.

'We are here, Miep,' I said. 'The house is on the left, number four.'

Miep slowed down and my eyes scanned the row of

houses, all with their neat white curtains. My eyes found the apartment where the Pomstras lived and as if by magic, Mrs Pomstra appeared at the window. I climbed stiffly from Miep's bike, and pressed the bell of the Pomstras' apartment. The door sprang open and we climbed the stairs.

My heart was pounding. How would I be received? Would they be happy to see me? I could see Mrs Pomstra standing at the top of the stairs. When I was about halfway up, she called, 'Is that you, Hetty?'

'Yes,' I answered.

'And your brothers?' Mrs Pomstra asked.

'They are okay, they're at Miep's house.'

I reached the top of the stairs. Mrs Pomstra said, 'How wonderful, my girl, that you are all alive because your father and your mother are alive as well.'

I reeled backwards under the impact of the shock, and Miep prevented me from falling down the stairs. I looked up at Mrs Pomstra, 'I don't believe it! You are not telling me the truth.'

'Come inside,' Mrs Pomstra said, 'and I'll show you the letters your parents wrote to us.' She put her arms around my shoulders and kissed me on both cheeks before guiding me inside.

Miep introduced herself to Mrs Pomstra and after I was seated on a chair, trying to control my shaking, Mrs Pomstra put three letters on the table in front of me. I recognised the letter I had sent from Belsen through the Red Cross. On the other two letters I recognised the handwriting of my mother and my father. I picked up my mother's letter first and with a shaking hand, I opened it. She had written to the Pomstras:

> *Dear family Pomstra, I am in Sweden in Malmö and I do not know where my husband or my children are. I think they are dead and I am alone in the world.*

She continued the letter in the same vein, in the belief that she was the only survivor. I then opened my father's letter. His letter was not addressed to the Pomstras. He wrote:

> *My dear wife and children, I am alive, I am alive and I am sure you are too.*

I burst into tears. The years of trauma, of deprivation, of horror and suppression all flooded to the surface as I read those words written by my wonderful, optimistic father. In his unshaken belief that we were all alive, the war had finally come to an end.

Hetty, sixteen years old, 1946.

Postscript

There was life after Belsen.

The Pomstras were beautiful people. They had a full house and we must have inconvenienced them at times, but there was never a cross word. Their hospitality was unsurpassed and their kindness helped to heal some of our pain.

Max went to Central Station every day. There he would read the list of names of those who had returned from the camps in Germany. Each time he would come home dejected, but the next day he would be off again in the hope our father or mother would return to us.

Then, in the first week of July, Mrs Pomstra told me that my father had arrived at Central Station. The doctors who examined him had transferred him to a hospital. Soon Mrs Pomstra and I were on the tram on our way to see my father. She told me that Max and Jacky had already seen him at the station and later in hospital.

A nurse directed us to the room where my father was

Jacky, Hetty and Max, 1950.

lying in bed, supported by pillows. I rushed up to him and put my arms around his thin frame. He looked so skinny. Tears of happiness filled his eyes and all he could say was, 'You have grown so much, Hetty.' We both cried. The feeling of relief that our ordeal was over left us without words.

When we had recovered, my father told me that he had been transported to Sachsenhausen, but after a few days he and another man had been separated from the diamond group. He had told Uncle Max to volunteer to join him but Max wanted to stay with the diamond group. This decision determined Uncle Max's fate — he died in Belsen.

My father was sent to a camp near Berlin. When the war came close the Germans took the entire camp on a death march. My father had to walk from Berlin to Mecklenburg-Schwerin, about two hundred and twenty kilometres. The march took a big toll on the hungry. When the prisoners could not continue to walk or dropped down on the road, the SS shot them without mercy. Dad managed to stay on the march for seven long days before they were liberated by the United States army.

On 3 June he had flown from Nüneberg to Brussels, Belgium, at about noon — we had missed each other at the airfield by only a couple of hours.

My father was a very sick man. His legs were swollen with oedema but after a few days in hospital, wild horses could not keep him away and he came home to the Pomstras.

Not being a person to sit home for long, he persuaded Mr Pomstra to find him a bicycle so he could go with Max each day to Central Station to see if my mother had arrived on one of the many boats coming from Sweden with refugees. The first few days we had to help him on and off the bike, and in order for him to stop and get off he used to wrap his arms around the light pole in front of our door to bring the bike to a halt. But after a week his health had improved and he was able to get on and off the bike by himself.

Months went by, and every day Max and my father would return from Central Station without news of my mother. We knew she was in Sweden but communication was still difficult in postwar Europe.

It was three long months before my mother finally came back. What joy, what happiness! She had put on an enormous amount of weight, as the Swedes had fattened up all the ex-prisoners. We hugged her and touched her every few seconds, and my father was on cloud nine now that he had all his family around him again.

My mother's transport from Belsen on 5 December 1944 had been sent to Beendorf concentration camp. There she had been put to work deep in the salt mines to build automatic pilot instruments for German planes. She was then liberated and sent to Sweden.

Amsterdam was dead. Food was scarce. There was no commerce and all the shops in the city were boarded up. Slowly, ever so slowly, things changed.

I returned to school but it quickly became clear to me, as well as my brothers, that studying was out of the question. We were still too mentally affected to concentrate. All five of us spoke very slowly and it was only after many years that our brainpower recuperated to the stage that we could speak normally again.

Fifty years after our liberation, 'The Children', as we called ourselves, had a reunion in Amsterdam to be once more with the woman who had so valiantly saved our lives in Bergen-Belsen.

Luba Tryzynska Frederick was awarded the highest decoration by Queen Beatrix of the Netherlands for Humanitarian Services in difficult circumstances.

Thirty-one 'Children' attended the reunion and the tears flowed freely. Although we were all fifty years older and had our own individual life experiences, we still, after all those years, quickly recognised and hugged each other and became the same close-knit group we had been in Belsen.

A fiftieth commemoration was also held at Belsen. I had no intention of going there ever again, but when (my little) Robby asked me to accompany him, how could I refuse? Robby was in a wheelchair; he had lost a leg from the after-effects of Belsen. Also, Maurice wanted to find Leni's grave, and I believed I could help him.

So I found myself in a bus on my way to the place which, at times, still gives me nightmares. The bus stopped and someone said, 'This is Bergen-Belsen.' There was absolute quiet. You could have heard a pin drop. This was the moment of truth, when we had to enter once more the gates of Belsen. Then the driver was told to continue on to another destination, and after about five minutes I realised that we had entered the recuperation camp. After fifty years the buildings looked the same, except that now there was no one about. It was clean and empty.

We went to the small cemetery in which Leni was buried — together with seventeen thousand others who died after the liberation from the effects of malnutrition and typhus, along with seventy doctors and nurses who contracted typhus whilst trying to help the poor victims.

As I alighted from the bus I noticed a much-decorated English military officer and a small man in a black suit standing next to the gate, and I walked up to them.

I asked the officer if he had been one of the liberators of Belsen. 'No,' he said, 'but this gentleman next to me was one of them. In fact, he was the young soldier who was sitting on the bulldozer pushing all those bodies into the mass graves. You must have seen it many times on TV.'

I was introduced to Frank Chapman, and before he knew it I put my arms around him and hugged him, and thanked him, after all those years, for liberating me. I had been unable to do so at the time as I had not been able to come out of my bed to meet the liberators.

Then Frank pointed out the one person in the crowd I had never forgotten. The image of his profile was engraved in my mind, and when I saw him after all those years I ran up and embraced him in the same way I had with Frank. I thanked and kissed, after fifty years, Dick Williams, the proud young soldier who was the first to enter Belsen with the white flag on 13 April 1945.

The solemn commemoration on 26 April 1995 took place in the grounds which were once Bergen-Belsen. The concentration camp is no more and only the silent mass graves tell the terrible story of what took place there during the barbaric regime of the Nazis.

I had great reservations about entering Belsen once again, but, surprisingly, it did not rekindle the horrors as I had imagined it would. Instead, it was as if all those mass graves were telling me: 'WE ARE AT PEACE NOW'.

The monument erected in Bergen-Belsen on 15 April 1946 by the ex-prisoners. 'Earth conceal not the blood shed on thee.'

Acknowledgements

I wish to gratefully acknowledge a number of individuals and organisations.

My thanks to my lawyer and friend Mr James Macdonald, for his encouragement to write this book; my friend, Mrs Joan McCreed, for her help and assistance with getting the book published; my publisher, Mr Ray Coffey, for his help and guidance.

My sincere thanks also to all my friends who have, over the many years, given me help and encouragement when, at times, the pain of recalling the past became too much.

My gratitude is also due to the Imperial British War Museum, Documentation and Archives Section, for the use of photographs.

About the author

Hetty Verolme was born in Belgium in 1930. In 1931 her family moved to Amsterdam, in the Netherlands. World War II broke out in 1939 and the Germans occupied the Netherlands. In 1943 Hetty and her family were sent to the Nazi concentration camp of Bergen-Belsen.

After surviving the war and working for a time in the fashion industry, she emigrated to Australia in 1954. She worked in many jobs, from waitress to bus conductress, from door-to-door retailing to selling real estate. Hetty eventually established herself as a successful shopping centre developer.

In 1972, Hetty was presented with the 'Most Successful Migrant' award. In 1977 she was appointed to the Australian Ethnic Affairs Council, and for many years she was actively involved in a wide range of community and charity organisations.

The Children's House of Belsen

Hetty is an abridged version of *The Children's House of Belsen*, first published by Fremantle Press (2000).

The Children's House of Belsen won the Fellowship of Australian Writers Christina Stead Award 2000. It has been reprinted many times and published in the Netherlands, Germany, Italy, France and the United Kingdom.

The Children's House of
BELSEN
ETTY E VEROLME

ALSO AVAILABLE

Sister Bullwinkel enlisted in the Australian Army Nurse Service at the outbreak of World War II and was posted to Singapore. In February 1942, she and hundreds of others attempted to escape the advancing Japanese army. The only survivor of the Bangka Island massacre, she was captured and held as a prisoner of war. Vivian spent the next three years working tirelessly to help her fellow prisoners. One of those prisoners was fourteen-year-old Edie Kenneison. Their remarkable friendship would help them survive and became the basis of a lifelong bond.

FREMANTLEPRESS.COM.AU